OLD HOMES, NEW LIFE

The resurgence of the British country house

TRIGLYPH
BOOKS

OLD HOMES, NEW LIFE

The resurgence of the British country house

Written by
Clive Aslet

Photography by
Dylan Thomas

CONTENTS

ΚΛΙ · Ο · ΛΟΓΟΣ · ΣΑΡΞ · ΕΓΕΝΕ

KAI · ESKHNOSEN · EN · HMIN

INTRODUCTION

By Clive Aslet

This is a book about twelve country houses. Many country-house books celebrate the subject's long history and ancient architecture; this one looks at a different aspect. How do people live in them today? How are these exceptional places, with all their splendours and inconveniences, their masterpieces and maintenance issues, faring in the twenty-first century? And what do they mean – to the owners, to the communities in which they are embedded, to the visiting public? The values of the age hardly seem to be in tune with ancient seats of privilege, filled with impractical furniture, and yet we remain gripped by the idea of the country house. What do the families for whom these extraordinary buildings are home make of the conundrum?

Once, a country house was the private domain of its lord, titled or otherwise, who filled it with guests and art treasures, and used it to project influence and prestige; nobody who was not invited got inside, except servants and family; but the sight of its battlements or spreading wings was well known to the local population, most of whom were housed quite differently. It was an image of dominance and authority. Not everyone would have understood the taste that it expressed but they would certainly have seen that great wealth was needed to build it. Privacy was part of the mystique. Most people could only guess at what happened behind its walls. Now country houses are rarely completely private (all my dozen open to the public in some way). Country-house visiting is an old pursuit, which goes back to the seventeenth century;

but before the Second World War, nobody expected it to make a significant contribution to running costs, as many owners do now.

We should not take public interest for granted. It is, indeed, almost perverse when you consider the history of these places. The people who built them, like so many benighted souls before the Year of Our Lord 2000, had hardly been enlightened by political correctness, which is of recent invention. Often enough the fortunes that built country houses came from tainted sources, involving embezzlement on a grand scale, or the selfish exploitation of the earth's resources. Industry polluted; the hugely profitable sugar economy of the West Indies ran on slavery; the corruption of the East India Company was legendary. Too much of the life supported by these ill-gotten gains was spent gambling, drinking, foxhunting and whoring. Wicked, very wicked. Of course, I write of past times. Gone are figures like the 15th Lord Saye and Sele whose profligacy in the first half of the nineteenth century caused every stick of furniture to be sold from Broughton Castle; when a new servant asked if he had any orders, he was told, as his lordship went into dinner: 'Place two bottles of sherry by my bed-side, and call me the day after tomorrow.' In this fallen age, there are fewer butlers and the stimulant of choice would not be sherry.

There are many cupboards in country houses, many skeletons. The #MeToo generation ought to be appalled. But the houses continue to capture the imagination of audiences at home and abroad. One hundred and sixty million people watch *Downton Abbey* in China. *Downton* stands in a tradition of country-house drama that includes *The Remains of the Day* and other Merchant Ivory films, as well as *Brideshead Revisited* and numerous Jane Austens. Although the world to which such period visualisations look back is outwardly quite different from our own, they are filmed in real country houses which, when the film crews have gone, will once again become family homes.

The country houses we see today are the survivors – ones that managed to stagger on through the dark times, avoiding the terminal consequences of wastrel heirs, dodging the worst of taxation and escaping the levelling tendencies of the twentieth century, during which as many as two thousand may have been demolished. They may have been traumatised by their experiences, perhaps losing wings and star works of art. They will certainly have morphed from what they were before the watershed of the First World War.

An Englishman's home may be his castle, sometimes – as at Helmingham Hall – with a working drawbridge which is cranked up every night; but even castles cannot keep out the representatives of the local authority and Historic England. A generation ago, acres of ancestral roof might be replaced – gratis to the owner, or with an only partial contribution towards the cost – by government grant: a reflection both of the impoverishment of ancient families and the historic importance of their homes. Those days have long passed. Economic conditions have changed; taxation is lower. But the State still helps, by exempting important objects and works of art from inheritance taxes in return for a degree of public access. (Though deferred taxes will have to be paid at their full amount if such pieces are sold, making sale a poor option.) The State also interferes. Statutory legislation to protect the fabric of important buildings (not just stately homes) means that they cannot be indiscriminately upgraded to meet the requirements of modern life. This only happens after a process of negotiation with officialdom. So we have a paradox: private properties that are not wholly private, packed with treasures that cannot realistically be sold; family homes that are also businesses; glimpses of rural paradise which will throw open their creaking gates for any event organiser that cares to pay to hold a wedding or rock concert.

It is obvious that country houses are different from other kinds of home. They are, to put it mildly, larger than the national average. Young children were romping in the kitchen of Loseley Hall when I visited; all part of normal family life, except that the young ones were dwarfed by the height of the room, which was twenty feet tall. One of the delights of being an eleven-year-old daughter of the Duke of Argyll is that you can ride a Segway around the basement corridors of Inveraray Castle (not allowed on the ground floor because it might damage the paintwork, but the basement is stone.) Unlike other homes, they are often shared with members of the public (warning to owners: change out of your pyjamas before they come). They are also very old.

Again, that might seem self-evident. It has struck me in a new light while writing this book. Ten of the houses I have included turn out, by complete chance, since this was not a criterion for selection, not to have been sold for five hundred years. The most recent arrivals are the Hopes of Hopetoun who came in the eighteenth century. It's not completely true to say that our country houses have been in the unbroken ownership of the same family. They often went down the female line – a fact disguised by the husband who married an heiress taking the family surname and sometimes title. A hiatus in the transmission of Doddington Hall came in the nineteenth century: beer brewed for young John Delaval's coming of age party is still in the cellars, since he died of consumption before the event, meaning that the house descended to a relation, Sarah Gunman. Sarah was about to marry, for the second time, when she too was carried away by consumption: as a testament to her love, she left Doddington to her fiancé – a dashing soldier. It went out of the family; but it had not been sold.

Half a millennium is by anybody's standards a long time: these country houses represent continuity on an epic scale. It is less surprising in Britain than elsewhere, where families such as the Grosvenors in Cheshire or the Clintons in Devon still own land that they acquired in the years after the Norman Conquest in 1066. On the other hand, many of Britain's biggest landowners are now not families, as would have been the case in nineteenth century, but institutions such as the Forestry Commission, the Ministry of Defence and the National Trust. In London, there are few if any houses, beyond the royal palaces, that are still owned and occupied by their eighteenth- or nineteenth-century families; hardly anyone lives in the same property as his grandparents. It is different in the country.

In 1982, Yale University Press published my book *The Last Country Houses*. It would have been better if I had stuck with my first thought for a title, which was *The Edwardian Country House*. Admittedly, in terms of the reign of Edward VII, the nine years from 1901-1910, did not quite fit the chronological range, since I was looking over a period from 1890 until the Second World War – a time of supreme comfort and, sometimes, wild creativity, in which the enormous fortune amassed from finance, commerce, armaments manufacture, oil, and South African gold and diamonds opened the door to fantasy, idealism and excess. The back of this movement was broken by the First World War.

In 1928, Noël Coward parodied the bankrupt state of country houses, as well as their idiotic and etiolated owners, in his song *The Stately Homes of England*.

> *Though the pipes that supply the bathroom burst*
> *And the lavatory makes you fear the worst,*
> *It was used by Charles the First …*

In *Operette*, in which the ditty first appeared, it was sung by the significantly named Lord Elderley, Lord Borrowmere, Lord Sickert and Lord Camp.

Most people, including Evelyn Waugh in *Brideshead Revisited*, thought that the Second World War had delivered the coup de grâce to this way of life. There followed a long twilight, as country houses struggled – or failed – to recover from being requisitioned by the armed services. The Victoria and Albert Museum's *The Destruction of the Country House* exhibition in 1974 catalogued a dismal toll of demolitions. Where new country houses were being built, they were part of managed retreat, providing a neat neo-Georgian box, perhaps on a site previously occupied by a larger edifice, into which the owner of a massive pile could downsize. Hence *The Last Country Houses …*

For it seemed to me then that the conditions that gave rise to country houses – Edwardian or otherwise – had gone forever. It was not that certain rich individuals could no longer afford to live on the scale of the plutocracy of previous ages, but the desire to do so had passed; hostesses did not want to be bothered with dozens of weekend guests, preferring to pack most of their visitors off to their own homes, easily accessible by motorcar, after entertaining them for dinner; the desire for privacy militated against employing the battalions of servants who would have been needed to run mega houses. There were exceptions, for whom entertaining was often seen as an extension of the business realm, but not many.

I should, though, have called my book *The Last Mammoth Country Houses*. Because since 1982 there has been a revival of country house building: admittedly not on the scale of loose, baggy monsters such as Tylney Court or Danesfield, built at the turn of the twentieth century, but gathering an ever-greater head of steam with the re-emergence of plutocratic super-wealth. In the early decades of the twenty-first century, which has witnessed the continuing rise of a global class of billionaires for whom owning property in the United Kingdom can be desirable both as a trophy to show off and an asset which their home government would find difficult to confiscate, it is almost as though Edwardian conditions are reasserting themselves. They do not always build enormous mansions but the money spent on revamping and enhancing old ones is astounding; a chapel alone may cost tens of millions of pounds. So I was wrong. *The Last Country Houses* was a poor choice of title. The breed survives.

The 1980s turned out to be a decade of some glory for the country house. It was a noisy time of Big Bangs and Lawson booms: good for those owners who could take advantage of the Loadsamoney coming out of the City of London. In 1985, the magnificent exhibition, *The Treasure Houses of Britain* opened in Washington, D.C., feeding a taste for the 'country-house look' – swagged curtains, fringed upholstery, 'tablescapes' (a word coined by the decorator David Hicks) – which not only colonised the drawing rooms of Manhattan but found an echo in the council houses that had been sold to tenants in Margaret Thatcher's property-owning democracy, their windows hung with festoon blinds.

Carried on the new political winds of the 1990s was a different attitude to the home. Chintz sofas and tasselled tiebacks blew out of the window. Into the vacuum came Minimalism.

The preferred building type was a converted loft or barn, rather than a country house. The long boom ended with the global financial crisis of 2007-08, but had generated the money for many country houses to be built.

And even this crisis did not restrain the appetite of some builders. If anything, those who had the money to create palatial homes did so on a bigger scale. Modern requirements have ballooned. Space is needed for contemporary art installations and collections of classic cars. Swimming pools are accompanied by spa suites and party barns. The master bedroom, with attendant closets, dressing rooms and bathrooms, may take up an entire floor. Space is a luxury and the rich want plenty of it. Country houses have an abundant supply.

Not that their traditional owners are generally in the league of super-wealth to which I have referred; if they have assets, they are difficult to get at. But they do not feel quite as isolated from their peers as their parents or grandparents might have done. They no longer see themselves as just hanging on, but as pursuing a way of life that others of their generation might be jealous of. For although restoration works are penalised by VAT, making them twenty per cent more expensive than new build, lots of dynamic individuals with money would like to take on an old country house. They may now be more likely to come from the worlds of software and biotech than the old guard, who typically had City backgrounds, but, according to Andrew Hay, Global Head of Residential at *Knight Frank* until 2020, they may be keener on architecture and gardening, and the environment now has a measurable value: 'Planting trees and restoring hedges can attract as much capital enhancement as having a two-bedroom cottage.' The families of the country houses in this book have been planting trees and restoring hedges for generations.

To keep an ancient country house going through the dark decades after the Second World War, when the country was on its knees, taxation high and labour expensive, required an all but obsessive devotion and focus on the part of those families who managed to do it. They exchanged the chance of a comfortable existence in London, or a manageable farmhouse, for a daily battle against antiquated plumbing, leaky roofs and dry rot. Even today, Helmingham's Victorian wing takes many days to heat up to an acceptable temperature; the surrounding moat does no favours on that score. Helmingham had been all but abandoned in the 1930s. Fortunately, the 4th Baron Tollemache who inherited after the Second World War was a businessman, able to contribute money generated from another source than the landed estate. But he had to start a dairy herd to get electricity installed – new lines could only be laid to agricultural units, not homes.

The doggedness with which impoverished aristocrats clung to their ancestral but practically uninhabitable piles would not have been easily understood in other countries. In the United States, hundreds of homes on the scale of country houses, often surrounded by their own land and farming operations, were built outside New York, Boston, Chicago, Philadelphia and other great cities between 1890 and the Wall Street Crash. Few of them were intended as dynastic seats. Owners rarely expected them to be occupied beyond their own generation. Mature trees were brought in, fully grown, to provide an instant landscape; the idea that a landowner would plant his park with timber that could only be enjoyed by his grandchildren did not exist. When the disaster of the Depression struck, taste moved on, and so did owners. Whole areas went out of vogue and the houses on them were demolished or forgotten. When I began work on a book on some of these dwellings, published as

The American Country House, some of my American friends refused to believe they had ever existed. They were too un-American to have done so.

By contrast, British families spend a large proportion of their incomes on buying property, tying up capital which is then unavailable for investment. Economists regard our love of home as an incubus (at life's banquet economists always count the potatoes.) But it runs deep. It is something that ordinary homeowners share with the inhabitants of the country house.

Certainly the sacrifices that were made by the post-War generation – and are sometimes still being made by their successors – to keep the family show on the road, and the family seat from falling down, are more explicable in Britain than in the United States or on the Continent. When the Depression hit Long Island, the Gatsby era houses were immediately abandoned, sold or demolished; they were not intended to be dynastic seats, passed down the generations. They were built for pleasure; their owners tended to frown on inherited wealth. In France, great families who were forced to economise in the twentieth century and faced a choice between a chateau in the provinces and a *hôtel particulier* in Paris unfailingly chose the latter. By contrast, British aristocrats chose their country houses over their town palaces, most of which were demolished in the 1920s and 1930s. This reflected the prestige of the country house in the UK. Italians would no more think of giving up their city life in favour of a castello on a mountaintop than they would fly to the moon (which is why so many remote rural properties can be eagerly snapped up by Danish, Dutch and British buyers, whose domestic dream is predicated on an absence of other people).

Today, the country house market is partly driven by a desire for privacy.

It is difficult for celebrities to keep their incognito on a London street, on which everyone's mobile phone has a camera. Absolute privacy, however, has never been easy to achieve, and it is not automatically available in country houses that need staff to run them. These days, many owners dislike employing staff, even when they can afford to do so. Who wants other people watching as you eat breakfast? Earlier generations treated servants with an emotional detachment that now seems brutal. The artist and versifier Edward Lear was one of the most delightful of people to meet in a drawing room; but he did not bother to discover even the most basic facts about his faithful servant Giorgio Kokali, with whom he travelled for several years. He was astounded to discover that he had a wife and family on Corfu, living in what turned out to be squalid conditions. I notice that the new generation of country-house owners prefer to employ young people – a butler of a tender twenty-four, in one case – rather than ancient retainers. They multi-task. They are more fun to have around.

Those families who managed to hang on live in happier times than their immediate forbears. Wives as well as husbands can take high-paying jobs (provided they are compatible with the sometimes onerous responsibilities at home). There are new sources of income on the estate. Weddings have been a boon: some country houses have proved such popular venues that the families, ironically, have moved out to live somewhere else – a case of tail wagging dog. Firle Park was being cleared for the filming of *Emma* when I visited (you can never have too many *Emmas*). Even the central heating radiators were being dismantled. The riding house has been converted to semi-permanent kitchens for television's *Bake Off: The Professionals* (a programme about competitive baking). Some owners insist that their homes, indeed, are not homes but businesses. They always have been.

What was a medieval coat-of-arms, asked one, but a logo? According to this view, country houses have always been corporate headquarters, from which families could run a host of self-enriching activities, from pillaging their neighbours to planting trees.

Well, perhaps. Country houses were often not built for domestic lives of the kind we would recognise. Our idea of home, based around families that live together in one place for most of the time, would have been alien to the aristocracy of previous centuries. They had many possessions; parents did not expect to see their children very much; dynastic marriages were apt to be fraught. A country house might have been built as an investment, since the owner would have hoped that his heirs and successors would live there after his time; he would have increased his income by improving his estates. But if one looks at the country house as a business, one can only say it is not a conventional one. Country houses are rarely very profitable. They may indeed run at a loss. These are not businesses that can simply be sold, lock, stock and barrel; family history and pride are involved. Nor is it possible for one that is struggling in a depressed area of the country to be lifted up and restarted in a more prosperous region. These days, estates are more efficiently run than would have been the case a generation ago (land agents are being replaced by CEOs), assets made to 'sweat', but I still detect a special pleading. The business argument is made because the public understands business, whereas the bonds formed by family history, generations of collecting and attachment to place are deeper waters.

Despite *Downton*, the populace at large finds country houses difficult to understand. Visitor figures to houses (not gardens) are falling. When Longleat and Woburn turned themselves into amusement parks after the

Second World War, the public flocked to them. There was little choice of entertainment. The idea that may have lingered in some minds that viewing the treasures of our nation's history was self-improving – good for the children. Now, people are more likely to go shopping. Old craftsmanship is not something to be marvelled at but lumped with the rest of the general category 'brown furniture' as something woefully out of fashion. Privilege is now hated. Deference is dead. Celebrities are the new aristocracy. Country-house owners who might once have been looked up to with a certain awe are now, in the public eye, regarded as weird. No wonder some of them want to present themselves as businesspeople instead.

The issues they face are, to the rest of the world, singular. Nobody wants to be the one dropping the baton. Family continuity can be seen immediately in the titles that are held by some of the owners in this book: at Grimsthorpe, the 28th Lady Willoughby d'Eresby; at Powerderham, the 19th Earl of Devon. Those whose lineage is not quite so unbroken will still want to pass on their inheritance to successor generations, preferably in better order than they received it. As the Devons reveal, this is another burden on the shoulders of the incumbent, whose blessings in life are accompanied by the weight of public expectation. People expect an earl or any other traditional owner of a big house to live up to the possibly romantic stereotype they have in their minds; celebrities and other rich people do not always subscribe to ideas of noblesse oblige – some use the excuse of security to shut the gates and avoid interaction with the community or wider public. So the said earl or traditional owner bears a weight of responsibility that can blight lives. And then comes the issue of transition. Many of the owners in this book (I use the term 'owner' loosely – the houses are often held in trusts) have recently come into their roles.

Their parents may still be alive and vigorous, but they have decided it is time for the next generation to have their turn. Parents then move out of the big house, leaving surroundings and possessions; children move in, usually making changes. This process is perhaps not so different from that taking place in other walks of life – family businesses, for example. It is always delicate, but a home is particularly fraught with sensitivities, associations and symbolism. Transition can be painful. Some owners just put it off.

Every family in this book has addressed this issue in its own way. Every family is different; every house is different. They are different in size, in wealth and in opportunity. Most of these houses are relatively little visited but a few can do well as tourist attractions. Some have more 'background heating' – in the form of money from outside the estate – than others. A house in the shires may make an income from shooting but that is not possible in Surrey, which is too populous. But affluent Surrey provides a ready market that does not exist in Cumbria. Some estates can dream of winning the lottery of life by obtaining planning permission for a housing development – although none of my examples has done so. For those in a National Park, like Firle, it is tantamount to being impossible, despite the best of intentions on the part of the owners. So there are differences; but also universals. One is the issue of primogeniture.

The principal reason that Britain has so many country houses, still in private hands and containing their historic contents, is that generation after generation has passed them on to only one heir. Almost invariably, this was the eldest son. The system of primogeniture was universally understood by the country-house owning classes and the world at large. On the Continent, with its different traditions, estates must be divided equally between family members, according to a proportion decided by law; this is the Code Napoléon. It is not the British way. But that way is being challenged by contemporary ideas. Why the eldest? Why son and not daughter? Or should not all the children have a share? (Assuming that the owner has children, which is not always the case.) Some owners stick with the old rule: rules have the authority of tradition. Others question it. Usually the choice falls on a sole heir, because the country house cannot generally survive if the estate supporting it is divided. But which potential heir is best suited to the task? And does he or she want to do it? It opens the way to unenviable family discussion.

Such questions arise because the fundamental values of the country house are not automatically those of the age. Life, powered by the internet, seems to be getting ever faster. Fashion changes more quickly, due to social media. News is instant but dies away as quickly as it came. Yet the country house stands for longevity and rootedness. This may sound old-fashioned but has positive benefits in areas of life that the public care about. Many of the prettiest villages around Britain are owned by estates, because the family in the country house have a long-term interest; they care about the places on their doorstep. The same is often true of the farmland and forestry on the estate; their natural capital is husbanded, because owners want to pass it on, in as best condition as they can, to their heirs. They expect their descendants still to be in possession of the estate in the next century, if not the centuries after that. Recently estates have proved to be far better at providing much-needed new homes in an attractive manner than the volume house builders, because the people who own the land known that they will have to live with the consequences, as will their heirs. They take a hundred-year view, rather than expecting to get a quick return.

They do not build, sell and move on. In this they have something to offer the modern world, caught as it is between the conflicting desires for instant gratification and sustainability.

One thing that links all owners is the knowledge that their time is short. Their tenure of thirty years or so will not seem long in the grand scheme of family history, and their family's association with that place. Nothing is certain. A wealth tax could be calamitous; although the country house might not be the specific target of such a measure, it would be brought down as collateral damage. For the moment, the barometer in the hall is set fair.

The country houses in this book are, in comparison to the domestic norm, peculiar; but they demonstrate a comforting notion: the importance of home. It is an idea that has echoed down the centuries, if anything getting louder in the present day. Households fragment: that is as true of the country house as other areas of life. But the country house remains a symbol of longevity, owned by families who, with some confidence, can expect that their descendants will continue to own and live in them many generations hence. The owners of the properties in *Old Homes, New Life* are staying the course. It is not always easy to do so. Turn the pages of the book and celebrate a continuing achievement.

House	Era	Family
Inveraray Castle Argyll	Georgian	The Duke and Duchess of Argyll
Hopetoun House West Lothian	Georgian	The Earl and Countess of Hopetoun
Hutton-in-the-Forest Cumbria	Medieval through to Arts and Crafts	The Lord and Lady Inglewood
Burton Agnes Hall Yorkshire	Late-Elizabethan; with Norman manor house	Simon and Olivia Cunliffe-Lister
Doddington Hall Lincolnshire	Late-Elizabethan	James and Claire Birch
Grimsthorpe Castle Lincolnshire	Early-Georgian	Baroness Willoughby de Eresby; Sebastian and Emma Miller
Helmingham Hall Suffolk	Tudor	The Hon.Edward and Sophie Tollemache
Madresfield Court Worcestershire	Medieval, mid- Victorian and Arts and Crafts	Jonathan and Lucy Chenevix-Trench
Broughton Castle Oxfordshire	Medieval	The Hon.Martin and Pauline Fiennes
Loseley Park Surrey	Elizabethan	Alexander and Sophia More-Molyneux
Firle Place East Sussex	Tudor and Georgian	Viscount and Viscountess Gage; the Hon. Henry Gage
Powderham Castle Devon	Medieval, Georgian and Victorian	The Earl and Countess of Devon

MADRESFIELD COURT

Worcestershire

Evie, Jack and Max Chenevix-Trench in the drawing room at Madresfield.
'We were very focussed on creating a family home,' says their mother Lucy Chenevix-Trench.

Lucy Chenevix-Trench's family have been at Madresfield Court, in Worcestershire, for nine hundred years. It may be this exceptional longevity that makes it one of the most romantic country houses in Britain; or is it the make-over that it was given in the Victorian period, which added turrets and hidden courtyards with élan – and little regard to the building that went before, except in preserving the moat? Readers of *Brideshead Revisited* will find it difficult not to see Madresfield through a poignant nostalgia for the period that Evelyn Waugh knew it, when the children of the 7th Earl Beauchamp had the house to themselves after the self-imposed banishment of their father, who had been outed by his brother-in-law, the 2nd Duke of Westminster, as a homosexual, and their mother's decision to return to her family home in Cheshire. Waugh, then in his late twenties, first went there in 1931. How blissful it was to enjoy the comforts of this fully staffed house with his young friends, although, as the novel attests, this heavenly state of existence could not survive the Second World War.

As an early exponent of the Victorian Revival, Waugh would have responded to the 1860s romanticism of the house. Madresfield was not, however – unlike some film representations of *Brideshead* – ostentatiously grand. Rather than making a powerful Baroque statement, with painted ceilings and a towering entrance hall, it is irregular and inward-looking, having evolved in what Lucy's husband Jonathan calls a 'somewhat random and organic manner,' as and when money permitted. While the Beauchamps had a big house in London, their Worcestershire seat was not surrounded by much of a park. Fields came almost up to the moat. The mile of drive that sails out towards the Severn Estuary in a straight line was only created in 1922.

Today there is one overarching priority at Madresfield, which is family life.

'We still have three out of four children at home,' explains Lucy. 'That will change, and as it does, priorities will change. But for now we both feel very strongly about its being a family home. There's such a profound meaning to the word "home". That has a huge influence on the way we live here.'

This was not, however, where Lucy grew up. 'The house was lived in by my great uncle and his wife; we visited once a year.' Lucy was twenty-three when her mother went to live there. The 7th Earl Beauchamp's heir, the 8th Earl, died in 1979, and subsequently his Danish widow, known as Mona, remained in possession of the estate; she was remembered by her *Times* obituarist for smoking ten cigars a day in a holder and riding a tricycle to overcome lameness. Her death in 1989 was followed by a lawsuit; fortunately, Madresfield came out of it intact, and Lucy's mother, Lady Morrison (granddaughter of the 7th Earl) moved in. Lady Morrison did a very considerable amount of work to the main rooms, but even so, when Lucy and John arrived in 2012 with four children – May, Jack, Evie and Max – under ten, they were faced with a significant challenge – the house had not had young children living in it for a hundred years.

'We were very focussed on creating a family home,' is how Lucy explains their response. The character of the house helped them. 'Moving into a very grand house would have been more difficult. Madresfield is not really grand; it is charismatic, a bit whacky, certainly unusual, and full of surprises – but in many ways an easy house to fit into. You can be yourself and fit into the spirit of the house and feel comfortable with it. You don't feel you need to live up to something.' Their most important change was to the kitchen, which was relocated away from what would have previously been staff passages, and into the main part of the house.

This was, says John, 'very important for the ergonomics of the house. Nowadays for most people the heartbeat of family life is in the kitchen. With the kitchen relocated, it is much more natural for us to use the wonderful main rooms, and the flow of the house is much easier. English Heritage and the planners were very understanding of this, and now the only disadvantage is that we don't use the front door as much – we do the school run from the back door.' This has the charm that the children leave across a covered bridge, whose windows contain stained glass quarries with their dates of birth.

'As soon as we unpacked a few bags it became home instantly,' recalls Lucy. 'The children made it much easier. And having not lived here as a child, I feel very much that we've been able to do this together; we were all new at the same time. In spite of being large, it's not a difficult house to live in. It's also a house where all the rooms get used. We don't have spooky bits that no one ever goes to.' When the children practise the piano, it is in the large staircase hall; that is also a space through which John walks as he goes from the kitchen to his office. The house has the further advantage of being 'quite far from London. We knew we couldn't commute. So this had to be home, with maybe one or two nights a week spent in London.' The children started off at local schools. 'I feel that the spirit of the house is a very good one; it's a house without an ego, which we rather like.'

But running Madresfield must be a complicated operation? 'It's not too bad,' says Lucy, 'and certainly no worse than for any other house on this scale. And most importantly we have the most wonderful team who all know the house incredibly well – we all work together.' From time to time they will fill the house with people. 'There were not a lot of guest bedrooms when we arrived,' says John.

'We found passages with lots of tiny bedrooms for visiting maids and valets – plenty of staff rooms but no staff to occupy them, sadly. They were full of stored furniture, and the bric-a-brac which accumulates after nine hundred years in the same house. We knocked down a few walls and opened the rooms up.' There are now twenty-four bedrooms. 'There's no point in having all these big reception rooms if you don't use them; you have to fill the place with people to make sense of it'. On Saturday, anything up to 40 people will be seated around the dining table. 'You feel that this is what the house is all about. These big houses need to be shared, and filled with people and laughter.' During autumn and winter, shooting parties are a good way of persuading people to make the long drive on a Friday night. 'We're often wondering about summer activities which could have the same effect.'

A huge amount of work went into placing furniture in the house. 'We had furniture from London and from our cottage near Hungerford, and with fantastic help from Todhunter Earle, we mixed these items up with what was already at Madresfield; we got a lot of dead furniture out.' says Lucy. 'We put stickers on everything. Some went on the bonfire, some went to the auction house, and then we carefully placed the rest. Some of the rooms at Madresfield had been quite dark; we wanted to lighten the place up, mixing the modern with the old'.

On the last Lady Beauchamp's death, the principal contents of the house had been made conditionally exempt from tax. In exchange for the waiving of inheritance taxes, the house must be opened to the public for forty days every year. Lucy did not know what she would make of it. 'With regard to the opening, both of us thought, "O my goodness, people wandering around in the middle of our house! We didn't have that in our cottage in Hungerford." Having now become used to it, we now feel there's a positive pleasure in sharing the house. It all works very well, and we learn a huge amount from our visitors.'

But there are also other ways of sharing the house. 'We're very keen on the ballet. There are so many pop-up operas in country houses – what about pop-up ballet? So we looked at the idea with the Birmingham Royal Ballet; with the requirement for sprung floors and other technical issues, it's a bit more complicated than we thought, but we are still looking at it. Meanwhile we've worked with them to offer retreats to artistic teams who are creating new ballets. They can come here and work together. They have occasionally danced in the staircase hall – but it's more an opportunity for the choreographer, composer, and dancers to spend time with each other on a project. Normally, a lot of their work is done remotely. To have a venue where they can get together can hopefully be helpful to them. It's a lovely thing for us and very much in the spirit of the house.' When the Three Choirs Festival is at Worcester, some of the programme is played at Madresfield. That reflects a turn-of-the-twentieth century connection, since Elgar, who played and conducted at the Festival, was a friend of Lady Mary Lygon, beloved sister of the 7th Earl.

And there's another project underway. 'We've recently become farmers,' says Lucy. For the first time in the history of the estate, the family are taking some of the farming in hand – about a thousand acres of the four-thousand-acre estate. 'It's not prime arable land but excellent for grass. We've established our first cattle, trying three traditional English breeds - Long Horn, Hereford and Sussex - to see which settles down best, and experiment with breeding.' The idea is to produce 'really top-quality, slow grown beef.

We'll just have them eating this wonderful grass that grows so well here.' This reflects a passion for the environment that is more than lip service. 'Our whole focus is on improving the environment. That starts with the soil. In this country our pasture and woods can play a vital role in addressing our carbon emissions, and non-intensive pasture fed animals are a key part of the cycle'.

A former senior figure in the City, John is now an entrepreneur working on various platforms in Africa and the UK. In spite of the enormous challenges of environmental destruction and climate change, he is optimistic. 'Attitudes are changing fast, albeit very late, and the challenges that we face will stimulate tremendous innovation and new technologies. Farming in this country will look very different indeed in ten or twenty years, and the environment will be the better for it. We want to try to make our small contribution to that process'.

Lucy is the twenty-ninth generation of her family to live at Madresfield, and with four young children, the likelihood is that there will be the thirtieth generation to take over at some point in the future. Both John and Lucy are very aware that ultimately they are just curators or guardians of the house and the wider estate. 'These estates and houses are an important part of the culture and heritage of our country; in an age when many aspects of our communities have been eroded, estates can contribute to rebuilding and sustaining rural communities. We'll do our best to make helpful changes and leave a positive legacy on what we have been lucky enough to manage. But in the end, we're just passing through'.

Window celebrating John and Lucy Chenevix-Trench's
twentieth wedding anniversary.

Previous spread, Madresfield Court, with the Malvern Hills beyond. The grass 'which grows so well here' now feeds a beef herd of Long Horn, Hereford and Sussex cattle.

This page, The Chenevix-Trench family – children Jack, Max, May and Evie, parents Lucy and John – in the hall at Madresfield, created by the art-loving 7th Earl Beauchamp with crystal balusters. A quotation from Percy Bysshe Shelley's *Adonaïs* is carved into the cornice: 'Shadows fly: life like a dome of many coloured glass stains the white radiance of eternity until death tramples it to fragments. The one remains, the many change and pass; Heaven's light forever shines.'

This page, Marble busts are displayed against
tapestry and panelling in the ante room.

Opposite, The panel above the fireplace is a word
puzzle on FREDERICUS installed by the 6th Earl
Beauchamp (whose Christian name was Frederick)
in 1890, the year before his death, to celebrate
the completion of the building project.

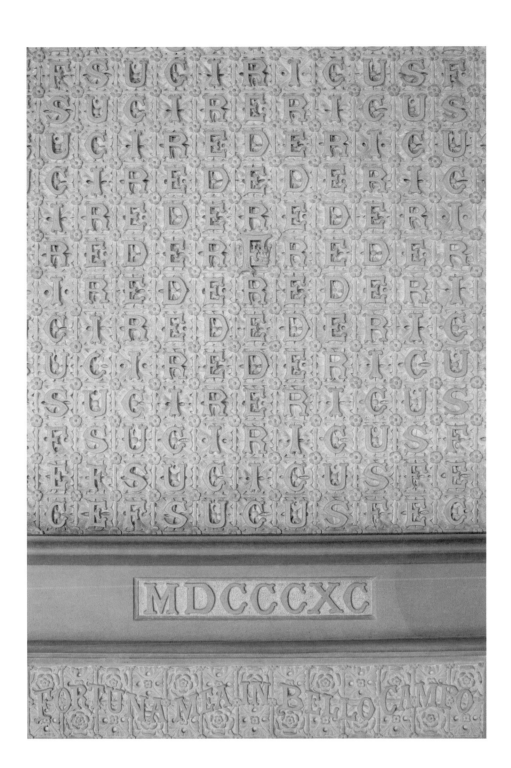

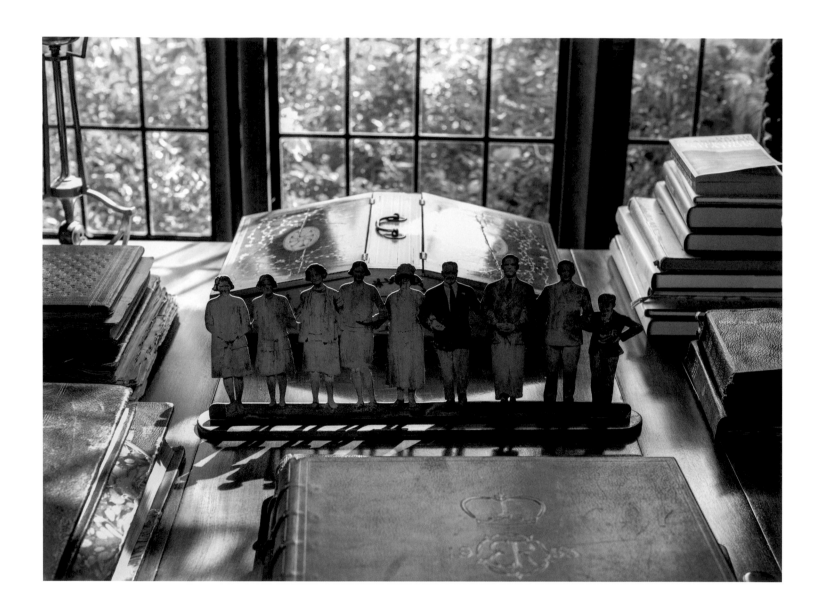

Cut-out of the 7th Earl's family. The children
were friends of Evelyn Waugh and an
inspiration for *Brideshead Revisited*.

The library, with bookstacks carved by C.R.Ashbee's Guild of Handicraft,
on a learned scheme devised by the owner. Work began in 1905.
The door carved with a crucifix leads to the chapel.

The chapel, given by Lettice, Lady Beauchamp to the
7th Earl as a wedding present on their marriage in 1902.

The work of Birmingham craftsmen, it is one of the most
successful and complete Arts and Crafts interiors in Britain.

Geese make their way to the moat, beneath P.C.Hardwick's Victorian walls; the little garden within the moat provides the family with sitting out space.

The family entrance, reached by a covered bridge.

OLD HOMES, NEW LIFE

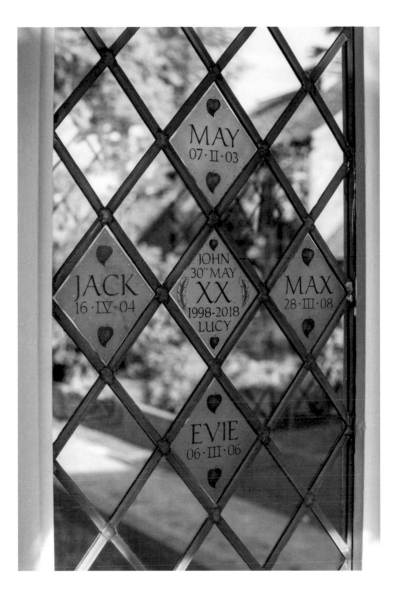

Opposite, Jack, the eldest son, born in 2004.

This page, Stained glass celebrates the children's birthdays ...
as well as remembering Madresfield's dogs and geese.

THE HISTORY OF
MADRESFIELD COURT

The same family has been at Madresfield Court, in the lee of the Malvern Hills in Worcesteshire, for nine hundred years. Little of the early house survives, though, since it was substantially rebuilt, on the old foundations in the 1860s. P.C.Hardwick was the architect, working for Henry, 5th Earl Beauchamp. Alas, Lord Beauchamp died of consumption in 1866, two years after work had begun. However, his scheme was continued by Frederick, the 6th Earl – 'very smart' and 'gaily dressed,' as Archbishop Benson described him – who would still be tinkering with the house twenty-five years later. The effect is magical. The bright red brick, the quaint Germanic gables and the bell turret added in 1875 give the impression of being lifted from the pages of a fairy story.

On its moated site, Madresfield could not spread in the manner of some Victorian country houses. Even so, Madresfield has a garden within the moat, formed in the crook of the house. Library and chapel stretch along its east side, with the long gallery above; the drawing room looks east and south.

The 6th Earl died in 1891, leaving an heir, William, the 7th Earl, who was equally committed to building – indeed, to all the arts. He had soon knocked two rooms together to form a new staircase hall. The balusters to the stair are made of quartz crystal, carved spirally. Two light fittings made of octagonal bands of opaque glass at right angles to each other used to proclaim the date, until removed by a twentieth-century owner: they were Art Nouveau.

Burke's Peerage charts the 7th Earl's outstanding record of public service: he was Lord President of the Council twice, Governor of New South Wales in 1899-1902, First Commissioner of Works in 1910-4, Lord Warden of the Cinque Ports in 1913-34, and Chancellor of the University of London in 1929, as well as Liberal leader in the House of Lords. But Lord Beauchamp had also an unusual sensitivity and a 'touch more of human tenderness,' noticed by the architect and campaigner for the simple life, C.R.Ashbee. The Earl embroidered upholstery and was an amateur sculptor of talent.

He and his wife Lady Lettice Grosvenor turned the library and chapel into a masterpiece of the Arts and Crafts Movement.

The library was extended to take in the billiard room, which was done away with – a statement of values in itself. Beauchamp must have admired Morris, having a complete vellum-bound edition of the Kelmscott Press. For the decoration of this room, Beauchamp chose Ashbee and his Guild of Handicraft as an expression of his informed and radical taste. Work on the room was underway by 1905 because on March 3 that year Ashbee wrote to Will Hart, one of the carvers of the Guild of Handicraft: 'Lord Beauchamp came down to the Court today, he seemed very pleased with the deepening results of the "Tree of Life" end, he is making an addition of another motto in Greek, which I should term swank, having already one in Latin.'

More generally, swank is hardly the quality one would choose to comment on in the room, as Ashbee himself would have been the first to admit. The contents of the shelves demonstrate several generations of learning and culture, and the reticent carving in low relief with which the doors and the book stacks are decorated appropriately enriches the repository of this family tradition. Ashbee's remarks show that Beauchamp was personally involved in devising the scheme which is learned and symbolic.

Lady Beauchamp had the chapel redecorated as a wedding present for her husband. While the library exudes a pleasant gravity, the only suggestion of colour coming from the bindings of the books, the chapel is radiant with flowers. On the east wall she is shown kneeling in her bridal gown in the attitude of a donor; Beauchamp kneels in his robes of state on the other side of the altar. Although work began soon after the wedding, it took so long to finish that the additional figures of the couple's children were worked into the design at the west end. Lord Elmley, the future 8th Earl, kneels with a broad-brimmed straw hat on his back, next to an angel; Lady Sibell and Lady Lettice sit on a carpet of flowers above this group, studying a book. The youngest brother Richard stands alone on the other side of the arch. On the opposite wall, Lady Mary and Lady Dorothy, the youngest sisters, are painted at the skirts of an angel in red, supposed to be their nanny.

Henry Payne painted the murals in tempera. With the reredos, altar frontal, metalwork, and stained glass, the chapel is a complete Arts and Crafts conception. In a small book on the chapel, presumably written by Payne (who certainly designed the wood cuts) and published in about 1907, the mood is described in characteristically mystical language: 'Through the open window steals the scent of blue-spiked lavender and jessamine with stars of white; the litany of gentle doves rises Heavenward to the music of the humming bees. The world without is glad with a thousand colours and a thousand songs, for every flower turns its face in praise of God, and every throat of things created has a song of Glory to His Name. And the walls within have caught the glory of that world outside …'

'Well I expect you must expect anything from a man that has his private chapel decorated like a barber's pole and an ice cream barrow,' wrote Ashbee to Will Hart, having just decried Beauchamp's wished-for show of Greek in the library. Evelyn Waugh's response was simply "Golly!" Now surely the chapel must be appreciated both for its beauty and as one of the very few places in which the ideal of a unity of the Arts and Crafts was achieved.

LOSELEY PARK

Surrey

Family al fresco at Loseley Park: Alexander and Sophia More-Molyneux
and their children, Cressida, Rocco, Aubrey and ZsaZsa.

'It's home.'

That, says Alexander More-Molyneux, is the meaning of Loseley Park, known to many people as a brand of superior ice cream, but – as the picture on the label shows – also a sixteenth-century country house near Guildford, in Surrey. Alexander and his wife, Sophia, have had two years there: time during which they have had to adjust to 'living above the shop,' as Alexander puts it, and their four children have overcome their anxiety sharing the property with strangers – between six and eight thousand members of the paying public each year. 'To begin with they were terrified,' says Sophia. 'They couldn't see them but they could hear them coming in and out. They don't really understand why anyone wants to come and look at the house anyway.' The number of days that Loseley opens has been scaled back as a result. The More-Molyneux are concentrating on other enterprises: gardens, weddings, wakes (they have a neighbour in Guildford Crematorium; my drive through the lanes to reach Loseley was preceded by a hearse). The ice cream business was sold in the 1980s. They want to do more with food, staring with the Farm Shop development which has just begun.

It is not only about market opportunities. 'We see one of the most important assets of the estate is the land itself,' says Alexander. 'When you look out of the window – there's a house called Loseley but also all this land.' The land – fifteen hundred acres of it – would cause a speculative house builder to salivate: it forms a 'green bubble' in one of the most prosperous areas of Britain, between Guildford and Godalming. All of it Green Belt and protected but still, one could hope. The family, however, sees it in quite different terms, which has little to do with monetary values. The land has always been there, owned, by the family, for more than five hundred years. It is part of their sense of home.

From Alexander's farming standpoint, it is 'not really good land. Chalk, sand, some clays – going down to loam with more sand. It's not easy to farm.' But the aim, particularly for Sophia, is to reach a level of environmentally sustainable production. 'What we feed our children is really important to us,' she says. 'That's where our plans come from.'

Historically, most of the estate has been tenanted but the More-Molyneuxs are now looking to increase the in-hand farming operation. The tenants are conventional farmers; in spring, the fields to either side of the drive are thickly buttered with the yellow, honey-smelling flowers of oil seed rape. 'We wouldn't buy the produce from the fields at the moment,' says Sophia. They intend to take some of the estate back in hand, for the family to farm themselves. 'We asked ourselves if we would do the same thing as now. We really wouldn't.'

So they are building a herd of English Longhorn cattle; a bull calf was born that morning. 'They're so beautiful, roaming these lovely fields. We hope they will feed us with wonderful beef.'

From the kitchen, an epic room with six-metre-high ceilings, comes the noise of four very robust More-Molyneux children, Cressida, Rocco, Aubrey and ZsaZsa – ages from three to seven. While not all of them will live at Loseley when they are grown up, the sense of there being a family connection which will endure long into the future is important here. 'Longevity' is a key word. They want to improve soil fertility and, says Sophia, 'boost our wildlife – we haven't seen a hedgehog for years. The house, weddings and all that will continue as a business, but we think that really what's important is the fruit and veg that are produced from our gardens. We live off it. Can we encourage other people to eat well?

This isn't a marketing tool. It's the right thing to do for us and we feel very strongly about it.' Recently they have obtained planning permission to convert a barn to a farm shop. It will sell beef that is only fed on grass. 'That means it has really good levels of Omega 3,' says Alexander. They will have lived 'as natural a life as possible.'

Alexander studied agriculture at Cirencester; afterwards, his first job was as a logistics manager for a ski company (Scott Dunn). Sophia has a degree in religious studies and anthropology from Edinburgh. They both spent a few seasons working in French ski resorts, and it was there that they met. 'I'd never heard of Loseley Park,' says Sophia, who grew up in the British Virgin Islands and Dorset. After France, she worked in public relations, before helping to open some shops in London.

Alexander's parents, Michael and Sarah, had twenty-five years in the big house; Michael continues to represent Her Majesty the Queen as Lord Lieutenant of Surrey. However, they had no difficult in moving out. 'Dad's happy in his new quarters. Their new house was remodelled in a nine-month project,' says Alexander. 'A total renovation. My mum is over the moon. It has underfloor heating. There are fewer stairs because the ceilings aren't so absurdly high as at Loseley. The rooms are very light; most of our windows are very high off the ground, specially in the kitchen, so the rooms are dark.' This left Alexander and Sophia to move into a house that, like any that has been occupied for generations, was already full of furniture. 'We had a lot of stuff from our previous house but my parents had also left things that they thought might be useful. It very quickly got claustrophobic in this big house.'

There have been few architectural changes.

'We ate in the kitchen when I was a boy,' says Alexander. 'We have moved the table, that's all.' Upstairs, Sophia says they could do with more and upgraded bathrooms; bathrooms at the ends of corridors have little allure. 'We like to have people to stay. It's fun for us. We find it is very difficult to leave Loseley; more often than not we have something going on here. We don't like to leave the house empty. If friends did not come, we would never see anyone.' One wing of Loseley is occupied by Alexander's grandmother Susan – great-granny to the children. Otherwise they use the whole house, though not all of it is regularly heated in winter; the temperatures are not those that Sophia remembers from the BVI. 'There are issues in keeping the house warm,' says Alexander with understatement.

Life at Loseley has been a learning curve. Sophia is becoming a gardener. 'We're about to plough a paddock for a flower garden. The whole of our own garden is now full of bare roots, waiting to be planted. I'm looking on YouTube every day to see where they can go. We've got some bees coming to occupy hives in the walled garden. We can't fit flowers for picking into the existing garden. The flowers will be good for the bees. The children are quite obsessed by insects.' It helps that Alexander's mother is a florist. 'She does all the flowers in the house during the open season and for weddings. I did a lot of research before choosing the flowers to go in and looked at the flower arrangements that I liked. I then ran the list past my mother-in-law and the head gardener. So I'm giving it a go.'

Weddings are a big earner for Loseley. Sophia likes them because of their structure. 'You know what's going to happen. One hundred guests in the great hall from 11am-12pm for the ceremony. You can plan your life around it, and it's always a happy event.'

But the number must be kept within bounds. 'We've met a couple of people who've experienced such a demand for weddings that they've moved out of their houses. We don't want that. They're lovely but that doesn't stop them from being a bit intrusive. I have to get children out of the house for an hour, or in front of a TV, while they're taking place.'

For now, the children go to local schools. Another line of communication is kept open by Michelle, the More-Molyneuxs' nanny. She grew up in Godalming and 'has a really good sense of what's going on there from her school years. They all keep in touch. We always know what's happening locally through Michelle.'

Unlike many country houses, Loseley does not have a shoot; it might not be popular in Surrey. While the children long for ponies, Sophia knows how much work they entail; 'we haven't got the time,' she says.

Who will take on Loseley in the next generation? That question will not need to be faced for some time, but an answer is already at hand: 'Whichever one wants it.' The eldest is a girl, followed by twin boys, then another girl. 'It would be obvious for it to go to Cressida, as the eldest. If she really didn't want it, then we'd have to think again. It's important for everybody to know where they stand.'

There is another thing about Loseley, and generally a subject about which English people are diffident. Weaving its way through the tapestry of family life is the golden thread of Christian belief. This is not overt; I would not have known of its existence if it had not been for a meeting in the tithe barn. When I asked what it was about, I was told 'Christian healing.' In any other age of Loseley's history before the Second World War, this would scarcely have caused comment: indeed, not to have professed faith in Christianity would have been more remarkable.

Today, the spiritual dimension of the house seems another part of the continuum with the past for which the country houses in this book are all striking. Religion is not a constantly burning flame. Alexander's grandfather was not specially devout until he experienced a vision. Since then it has been part of the shared family identity.

So near London, Loseley seems to define itself by its difference from the metropolis. London is a hustling, changing, ever-enthralling city, throbbing with the excitement of new arrivals, new experiences, new thoughts. Loseley is a symbol of the long term. Alexander and Sophia are themselves excited to be 'starting a chapter in our lives in our family home; deciding what we want to achieve and how we can make it happen.' Doubtless the house will be reinvigorated by their contribution to its history and set on a good course for the future; but its old stones will not change much during their era. As Alexander remembers his grandfather saying, 'Loseley shrugs its shoulders as each generation comes in because it knows it will outlast them.'

Alexander and Sophia More-Molyneux, with Bracken, in front of a fireplace of about 1610.
The lower part is carved from chalk; the plasterwork above is decorated with
martlets and cockatrices, emblems of the Jacobean Sir George More and his wife.
Alexander is descended from the Elizabethan builder of the house.

Previous spread, Loseley was built in the 1560's of local, tobacco-coloured, Bargate stone, some of which came from the ruins of Waverley Abbey after the Dissolution of the Monasteries. The Baroque doorcase dates from about 1689.

This page, The Elizabethan great hall contains decoration from Henry VIII's palace at Nonsuch. The panelling combines splendidly with the great early-eighteenth century portrait of Sir More Molyneux, whose wife Cassandra bore him eleven children.

This page, Twins Rocco and Aubrey face up to each other in the old scullery maids' passage, now the entrance hall for the family; the doorway on the right leads to the kitchen.

Opposite, The centre of family life is the tall Elizabethan kitchen, stripped to its ancient brick; Alexander supervises homework.

In the drawing room, whose ornate Jacobean chimneypiece is carved in chalk. 'When you look out of the window,' says Alexander, 'there's a house called Loseley but also all this land.' Nurturing the fertility of the estate is a major focus.

Opposite, Chippendale glazing on a china cabinet in the great hall echoes the leaded lights of a window.

This page, Tapestry hangs behind a Georgian four-poster bed. The More-Molyneuxs like to have friends to stay, because Loseley's busy schedule means they can rarely spend time away from the house.

This page & opposite, Inspecting the herd of English Longhorn cattle that has been recently established. 'They're so beautiful, roaming these lovely fields,' says Sophia. 'We hope they will feed us with wonderful beef.' The estate is a 'green bubble' between Guildford and Godalming.

Every good house must have an attic. This one doubles as a carpentry workshop.

THE HISTORY OF
LOSELEY PARK

The History of Parliament describes Sir William More as 'the perfect Elizabethan country gentleman.' He was not, however, as retiring as that description makes him sound. Moving in the highest circles at court, and so friend to many of the leading figures of the age, More was also an MP, Sheriff - later Deputy Lieutenant - of Surrey and Sussex, Vice Admiral of Sussex as well as serving locally as a justice and commissioner. The Queen herself had an excellent opinion of him. When More's house of Loseley Park was finished in 1568, she lost no time in visiting him; she was there in 1569 – she may have gone as early as 1567. It was on the route of her progresses in 1576, 1583 and 1591. Through his daughter Elizabeth, who was one of the Queen's ladies at court, and her husband, the Latin Secretary John Wolley, he was kept abreast of court life. Wolley told his father-in-law how the Queen had fallen 'in speech of you, with great good liking and commendation.'

In 1595, More attended Queen Elizabeth on one of her progresses and had difficulty returning to Loseley. Elizabeth Wolley wrote of the Queen's concern over the 'troublesome' journey he had been forced to make after dark: 'If her Majesty had known ... she would have had a lodging provided, being likewise sorry that she had no longer time to entertain you'. The Queen sent him three partridges, 'desiring you to eat them for her sake'; in the event, they never arrived, because Sir Robert Cecil, whose hawk it had been that killed them, took them instead. So More had to pretend to the Queen he had received them.

There had been an earlier house at Loseley but it was not on a scale to welcome the monarch. It seems that the old house was kept for some time after the present Loseley was built, to be used as lodgings for guests. One such guest wrote to Sir William that he would be happy to furnish his own chamber 'with beds, hangings and all that thereto belongs' – on the principle that owners did not always furnish guest accommodation. Eventually the old house was demolished.

Work on the new Loseley began in 1561 when timber was being bought. Some of the stone was dug from the ruins of Waverley Abbey, 'out of the rubbish' as one of the entries in the accounts has it. By 1568, it was possible to glaze the windows, using eleven cases of glass; More's coat of arms in the oriel window of the hall is still there. The principal mason was called Mabbanke, according to the building accounts. A survey by the architect John Thorpe, now in Sir John Soane's Museum, shows a courtyard entered by a gatehouse. What remains today is a single block, always the one containing the grand rooms, facing north towards the Hog's Back. There are seven gables, of unequal size; of the two inner bays, one contains the porch, the other the oriel bay to the hall. Over the porch are carvings that More had sent from London. The asymmetrical front garden reflects with requirements of the plan, with a nursery wing added to the southeast in 1877.

More was not only enriched through his position at court. In 1559, he received a substantial bequest from his friend Sir Thomas Cawarden, which included some valuable houses in London – built on the site of the demolished Black Friars monastery in London, which Cawarden had received from Henry VIII at the Dissolution. Cawarden was in high favour with Henry, who made him Master of the King's Revels, Keeper of the King's Tents and Keeper of the Palace of Nonsuch. It may have been from Cawarden that Loseley now has the series of painted grotesques known as the Nonsuch panels. (Another theory is that they arrived when Nonsuch was demolished around 1680.) They include panels in the great hall, inlaid with trompe-l'oeil arcades with chequerboard floors in dazzling perspective. In the Surrey volume of *The Buildings of England*, Ian Nairn and Sir Nikolaus Pevsner describe them as 'superbly done,' Nonsuch being 'a repository for most of the advanced ideas of the 1540s ... a mad scramble to put up a world-beater by a king as voracious for the

biggest and most up-to-date as any American tycoon of the 1890s.'

More died in 1600, to be succeeded by his son, Sir George More. Sir George was, like his father, a politician and courtier. He entertained James I at Loseley and in 1615 became Lieutenant of the Tower of London – a 'troublesome and dangerous office' that he sold after two years. At Loseley he built a new wing, possibly to the design of Thorpe. This wing was demolished in the 1830s, but Sir George's hand is probably to be seen in the spectacularly sumptuous chimneypieces with their fantastic figures and exuberant detail in the dining room and drawing room – the latter being carved in chalk. Since Sir William More's otherwise extensive accounts are silent about decoration, we can assume that his house was relatively plain. The chimneypieces incorporate the More device of a mulberry tree, that being a pun on the family's name: the Latin for mulberry is morus. Sir George More's daughter, Ann, secretly married the poet John Donne, then a notorious libertine (though he would later become Dean of St Paul's); Sir George got him imprisoned.

The early Georgian owner, Sir More Molyneux, who succeeded in 1719, can be seen in the large family portrait in the great hall; his wife Cassandra bore him eleven children. Surrounded by a splendid Baroque frame, bearing a coat-of-arms, the painting was presumably made for this position – one of the many works undertaken by Sir More to Georgianise the house.

Loseley survived the nineteenth century without much alteration. Around 1880, it was let to the North American lawyer, financier and politician Sir John Rose and his wife Charlotte. They were friends of Henry James who visited them at Loseley. He may have drawn on it for his picture of Gardencourt in *The Portrait of a Lady*.

HELMINGHAM HALL

Suffolk

The Hon. Ed and Sophie Tollemache in the drawing room at Helmingham Hall in Suffolk.
The house was decorated by Ed's parents with the help of David Mlinaric.

There is a mechanical whir, followed by clanking. The drawbridge at Helmingham Hall is going up. One of the drawbridges, I should say – there are two of them, just as there are two moats: one around the house, the other around the celebrated garden. 'You do feel safe when the drawbridge is up and the doors are locked,' says the Hon. Edward Tollemache – Ed to most people on the estate – who has recently moved into Helmingham. Fortunately, it is no longer necessary to crank the drawbridge into the vertical position by hand, using the system installed in the nineteenth century. But the door that closes behind the portcullis has not changed. Decorated with carved tracery and studded with metal bolts, it dates from the early Tudor period when the house was built.

Helmingham has come down from that time, complete in all its parts. You see it first, as a flush of rosy brick, at the end of an avenue of ancient trees, their successors – since these veterans are nearing the end of their lives and some were blown down in the 1987 hurricane – already growing beside them. Deer graze the four hundred-acre park, as they have always done. Untouched for hundreds of years, Ed calls it 'our own wildlife sanctuary'. Two fishponds known as the Leys survive from an era when they supplied fish to the Helmingham table. A trio of oaks known as the Three Sisters, misshapen with age, still clings to life after seven or eight centuries of existence. This Suffolk countryside is flat; the house is long and low, its silhouette enlivened with fanciful chimneys and finials. For a place of such age, such beauty, to survive in the hands of the family who built it is, surely, a species of English miracle.

Those hands, in the present (twentieth) generation, belong to Ed and his wife Sophie. They and their young family – Ralph, Theo and Stella – came in the summer of 2017.

Ed is one of three siblings, but 'had always known I was in line for it.' This was not the result of a formal briefing from his parents; he simply picked up the idea – just as his elder sister Selina and younger brother James must have realised that the home in which they had grown up would no longer be theirs. 'I don't think Helmingham or many estates like this would be here if they were continuously divided up on inheritance,' says Ed. The transition was planned with his parents, Tim, 5th Baron Tollemache, and Xa, dressage rider turned professional gardener, in 2012, five years before the move took place. 'Sophie and I got married in 2007,' says Ed. 'We never really spoke about moving into Helmingham until 2010. Two years later we had more of a formal chat with my parents. Dad was the Lord Lieutenant of Suffolk. Lord Lieutenants are the county representatives of Her Majesty the Queen and have quite an intense role. Dad has a strong sense of duty – it's really honourable. He was due to retire in 2015 and quite understandably wanted a bit of time when not Lord Lieutenant to enjoy Helmingham. We arrived over the summer of 2017 so the children could start school locally in September.' Ed himself was sent away to board in a distant county – Wiltshire – at the age of seven. Like many other modern couples, Ed and Sophie feel this is too early; they are as yet undecided on whether the children will board at thirteen.

Ed remembers that the 'first few conversations were probably the hardest. It was quite difficult for us to talk about it. By the time the move happened, it wasn't difficult at all because we had got so used to it. We all knew what was happening. It wasn't awkward but it wasn't easy. Moving into a place like this shouldn't be particularly easy.' Other challenges were to come. 'The hardest thing was being in the house without my parents-in-law,' says Sophie.

Working first in television, then corporate intelligence, she had become used to visiting with Ed, and finding a super-comfortable, welcoming family home. 'The day they moved out was very sad.' She realised that she was now the chatelaine. Xa, however, had some sage advice. 'You have to fill the house with your friends again and again and again.'

Tim and Xa's new home is at Framsden, where they had lived very happily after their marriage in 1970; they were snatched from this comfortable, historically interesting farmhouse in 1975, when Tim's father, John, the 4th Baron, unexpectedly died and it was their turn to inhabit Helmingham, with all its antiquity and challenges.

John Tollemache began the revival of Helmingham, having inherited the estate from a cousin in 1955 – a dark era for country houses, still suffering from the privations of the Second World War. Guests who stayed there remembered toothpaste freezing in the tubes. When the Eastern Electricity Board would not run a cable to the house, John Tollemache hastily founded a dairy herd to take advantage of the priority being given to agriculture. Times changed and Helmingham blossomed, literally so in the case of Xa's garden. Before her arrival, the garden had been used principally to grow vegetables. 'I was twenty-two and didn't have a clue about gardening,' she remembers. But she took a spade and asked Roy Balaam, the head gardener who has now worked at Helmingham for over sixty-two years, to instruct her in digging. (Later she even mastered the skill of driving a JCB – wonderful for earth moving.) By 1996, she had conquered the subject sufficiently for Max Hastings, then editor of *The Evening Standard*, to commission her to design a classical garden for the Chelsea Flower Show. It won a gold medal. In 2017, Helmingham, whose gardens are open to the public from May to September, was made the Historic Houses' Association Garden of the Year, in an award sponsored by Christie's.

Sophie is now studying with The Plant School but she and Ed were delighted when Xa offered to stay involved. This typifies their attitude to the house. 'We're very settled here now but it has taken us a couple of years to work out how to live here, what we want to change and what we don't.' Dylan's photographs for this book pay homage to Tim and Xa's years at Helmingham, as much as the new generation. Helped by their friend David Mlinaric, Tim and Xa created a series of interiors of timeless sophistication and charm. Ed and Sophie see no compelling reason to change them. They're lucky, too, in the house itself. When it was Georgianised by the 4th Earl of Dysart in about 1750, the low-ceilinged proportions of the Tudor house were preserved. This may have been a source of regret to the architect: the Corinthian columns, scroll-headed pediments and Classical busts of the 4th Earl's library, now a drawing room, could have used more room to breathe. But they have bequeathed a series of grandly conceived rooms, executed on an almost cosy scale – and now decorated with ineffable taste. These are not unapproachable spaces. 'Everyone who comes here says that it's like a family home,' comments Ed. 'If we can carry on getting that feeling, we're doing okay as that's exactly what it still is.'

On my first visit, a very long oak table is being manoeuvred, with difficulty, into the former billiard room. Six people are needed to move it. By the time I return, it has already served well for shoot lunches, while the room that the table came from has been transformed into a family sitting room, with sofas and a wood burner. When the previous carpet was lifted, it revealed a hitherto unsuspected floor of old brick. Heating in the children's bedrooms has been improved – although the big rooms created on the west front, overlooking the garden, for the 1st Baron Tollemache's large Victorian family still take a fortnight to raise to an acceptable temperature during winter. (Absence of radiators is a boon for the furniture: drawers in the walnut and tortoiseshell cabinets open and close 'like a Rolls-Royce.' For preservation's sake, the curtains are also kept closed.)

Fred and Percy – a Dachshund and Shitzu-poodle – are now ensconced in the house, along with a Leopard Gecko called Isaac. An established events business is being developed, to supplement the estate's prime income generator of farming. A winter illuminated garden trail, launched in 2018 has seen numbers grow from 2,000 to 9,000 in its sell-out second year. 'We wanted to celebrate the gardens at a time they're normally closed. It's a magical, enchanting family event and one we're very proud to host'. A house manager and nanny live in the house, supported by a housekeeper and part-time daily. Gone are the 'series of ancient retainers' of past generations.

The most pressing need is to convert the kitchen, large but impractical, into a more friendly space. If a window could be converted into a door, it might lead into a conservatory; the house, as the home of a light-loving family who enjoy watching the sun set from a strip of terrace by the moat, would be transformed. At present, the eating rooms are all some way distant: 'That doesn't make sense when you're trying to get children dressed for school, having breakfast, packing bags, doing homework. It's nice to be all in one room.' Eventually, a new use might be found for the stables, which no longer contain horses.

Taking on a house such as Helmingham is not for the faint-hearted. It can be particularly daunting for the owner's wife – as Sophie will attest. She grew up in London, a child of BBC parents, one a script supervisor, the other a producer. For the mother of young children, life in Battersea, the Tollemaches' previous home, was appealing. 'There was, oddly, a more obvious community in London. For the forty minutes that I was on the school run, I was always bumping into neighbours and other mothers. You got used to being closely surrounded by people whose company you enjoyed. In the country, you have to get into the car and everything is more spread out. We've made some great friends and the community is there, you just need to work a bit harder to find it.'

On Mondays and Fridays, Ed works from Helmingham. Sophie joins him in running the estate. 'During the winter, people stay in the house for the let shoots; everything has to be perfect. In the summer, we focus on the events business. I'm getting to grips with understanding the other areas of the estate, such as the property side – though not the farming; I leave that to Ed.' The division of labour would have surprised earlier generations.

What does Helmingham mean in the modern age? Ed is definite. 'It means continuity and stewardship. It also means being brave to ensure it evolves around you and your family and not being afraid of change. It's sometimes strange to think that we'll only be here for thirty or forty years while it's been here for well over five hundred. That's not a very long time in the grand scheme of things. If it can stay in the family for the next five hundred years, then we will all have done a good job.'

The quiet and ancient beauty of Helmingham Hall.
The hall was refaced by John Nash around 1800,
hiding Tudor half-timbering beneath brick and
mathematical tiles; Nash also added the oriel window.

Ed in the Boudoir with his children Theo, Stella and Ralph. The 4th Earl of Dysart's architectural decoration of about 1750 was adapted to existing Tudor proportions, making a room that contrives to be both grand and cosy.

Opposite, The great hall, created in the 1840s;
it incorporates old pieces of carving, for example
in the columns flanking the fireplace.

This page, A rather forbidding room comes
to life when children use it.

This page, Thought is being given to the kitchen, which is too far from the rooms where most eating takes place.

Opposite, Theo with ray gun.

Beneath rows of Victorian servants' bells, Ralph prepares to go for a ramble. When the old carpet was recently taken up, the old brick floor was revealed.

Previous spread, Helmingham's low lines reflect those of the Suffolk countryside in which it sits. Xa Tollemache's famous garden is contained within the outer moat. Helmingham has been fortunate that new work has always been sympathetic: the wing facing the camera is Victorian.

This page, Xa Tollemache continues to look after the garden that she created, although her daughter-in-law Sophie now goes to The Plant School to learn about horticulture.

Opposite, Helmingham won the Historic Houses' Association Garden of the Year award in 2017.

In the park. Grazed by deer, as it has been for four hundred years, it is, Ed says, 'our wildlife sanctuary'. Some of the trees are older than Helmingham itself.

THE HISTORY OF HELMINGHAM HALL

The Tollemaches were probably originally Norman. They obtained the first of their lands at Helmingham through marriage into the Joyce family, who had bought it in 1386. It has never been sold since.

Before today's house was built, an earlier one called Creke Hall stood on the site. There are two medieval moats, one surrounding the house and the other defending, presumably, a farmstead with barns and livestock. Creke Hall was entirely replaced by the present building. This was the work of John Tollemache, who inherited from his father Lionel in 1511. It takes the form of a quadrangle. The hall was opposite the gatehouse with the most important family rooms to the west. This layout survives, although in one respect the Tudor house would have looked quite different from today. While the hall range was built of brick – a favourite Tudor material, newly reintroduced to England and capable of much caprice in the twists and ribs of the chimneys – the entrance front was half-timbered. A glimpse of this can be seen in an inner wall of the gatehouse, where the studs are still visible.

Despite its immemorial appearance, Helmingham was refashioned in three separate campaigns of work during the eighteenth and nineteenth centuries. Around 1750, the 4th Earl of Dysart remodelled the Tudor house. The Dysart title had been acquired from beautiful, witty and extravagant Elizabeth Murray, whose father, William, had been whipping boy to the young Charles I; as a Prince, the future King could not be beaten and so his punishments were taken vicariously by his friend, who was later made Gentleman of the Bedchamber and an Earl. The earldom was only confirmed during the Restoration when Elizabeth acquired a new patent, with the provision that the title could descend through the female line. In reaction against the profligacy of his mother, the 2nd Earl had been frugal and refused his eldest son an allowance; in later life, that son, the 3rd Earl, continued the parsimonious habits that he had learnt in youth. So when his grandson, the 4th Earl, came into his inheritance, the coffers were full.

As well as Helmingham, Lord Dysart now owned Harrington Hall in Northamptonshire, Woodhey Hall in Cheshire and Ham House outside London. Nevertheless, he was also cautious, as can be seen from the meticulous accounts that he kept – down to the halfpenny he gave to a boy for opening a gate.

A more extravagant man might have rebuilt Helmingham: the 4th Earl was content to remodel it, hiding the timber frame beneath brick and mathematical tiles, inserting sash windows and giving a parapet to the roof. Inside he created a new staircase, with twisted balusters; a large kitchen; and a series of rooms in the south-east corner of the house (others do not survive), decorated with columns and pediments in the latest taste. Despite having travelled on a Grand Tour, he was content to adapt the Georgian fittings to Tudor proportions: as a result his rooms manage to be both grand and intimate at the same time. One of his rooms was a library for his many books, some transferred from Ham House. No architect is mentioned in the 'Suffolk Accompts' kept by the Earl's Steward.

The 5th Earl – 'a very handsome person,' according to Horace Walpole – reverted to a previously established family type, by becoming careful with money. He had Harrington and Woodhey comprehensively pulled down and their gardens ploughed up. When George III intimated that he might drive over from Windsor to breakfast with him at Ham, Lord Dysart returned the reply: 'Whenever my house becomes a public spectacle His Majesty shall certainly have the first view.'

The 5th Earl died without children. His brother, Wilbraham, the 6th Earl of Dysart, was a different character. An army officer and an MP, he was sixty when he inherited – an elderly man in a hurry to spend. As well as buying land and creating the Yellow Satin Bedroom at Ham, he employed Nash to improve Helmingham, which had become too plain for the Picturesque taste of the Regency. Accordingly, Nash added an oriel over the entrance gateway, finials to its gable, crenellations to the parapet and replaced the 4th Earl's sash-windows with mullions and Tudor dripstones. Nash was also responsible for the pretty iron bridges over the moat. His designs were exhibited at the Royal Academy in 1800.

Admittedly sharing Humphry Repton's aversion to red brick, as forming too warm a note in a landscape, Nash had Helmingham's rose-coloured walls plastered with stucco, no doubt to imitate stone. Otherwise, he made it both more charming and more seemingly ancient. The artist John Constable, a favourite of the family, roamed the park freely whenever he wanted to paint it.

On the 6th Earl's death without children in 1821, Helmingham passed to Lady Jane Murray, who removed the stucco that her brother had applied. It was her grandson, John, who became the 1st Baron Tollemache.

In architecture, the 1st Baron Tollemache is remembered for creating Peckforton Castle, a genuinely convincing and deeply chivalric castle on a sandstone outcrop in Cheshire. But having taken the title of Tollemache of Helmingham Hall, he must also have had an affection for the family seat: he upgraded it, adding rooms that would be big enough to accommodate his extensive family. His eleven surviving sons – there had been twenty-four and one daughter, by two wives – could field their own cricket team. Helmingham's west wing, next to which there had previously been a herb garden (the kitchen was nearby), was rebuilt, probably by Anthony Salvin, the architect of Peckforton. Lord Tollemache reigned at Helmingham for half a century, a staunch Tory and paternalistic landlord. Subsequent generations have done little to alter the house, beyond making it prettier inside, as well as more comfortable.

BURTON AGNES HALL

Yorkshire

Islay, Inigo, Otis, Joss and Sholto Cunliffe-Lister in front
of Burton Agnes Hall, in the East Riding of Yorkshire.

'I think the house is the sum of the involvement of so many thousands of people over more than four centuries, and going back further than that,' says Olivia Cunliffe-Lister. She is the chatelaine of Burton Agnes Hall, in the East Riding of Yorkshire; her husband Simon's family have been living there by descent, sometimes through the female line, since it was finished in 1603. Immediately next door is one of the earliest domestic buildings in the country, a Norman manor house. She continues: 'I ponder the vast number of people who have been involved at various stages – planning the creation and ongoing custodianship of this very, very special house. If one considers the original craftsmen who would have carved every piece of this room that we're sitting in; the people who would have set the fires in every single room in the house; all the cleaning over the years; the way that the house was a community composed of ancestors, guests, associates – so many people in the present and the past have a stake in the house. They've given it their time, energy and life. To me, it holds all that. Not exactly the ghosts of the past but it brings together the endeavour of a huge community of souls. I feel we're maintaining the legacy of all that, and we must tread extremely carefully because we're treading on people's past.'

You don't have to be at Burton Agnes very long to know what she means. It's as delicate as a moth wing, as poignant as a pressed flower. You may not see the ghost of the Jacobean lady, except in a painting in which she features with her two sisters (it is a posthumous portrait of her: she wears black); but it is easy to believe in her presence. Burton Agnes is little changed since the eighteenth century. The great hall could have been finished yesterday; carved and plastered with a host of figures – Biblical, allegorical, mythological – it appears to have been conceived on a theme of authority and punishment.

Sir Henry Griffith, who began the house in 1598, was a Member of the Council of the North, which imposed justice on the northern counties; presumably the decoration was intended to reinforce his position. And yet it is not a gloomy house. Anything but. Simon and Olivia have five children – Islay, Joss, Otis, Inigo and Sholto – and the exuberance is inescapable. This is the first time for nearly a century that Burton Agnes has echoed to the sound of youngsters. It's a great place for hide and seek.

Simon inherited Burton Agnes at the age of twelve. That was in 1989, on the death of his remote cousin Marcus Wickham-Boynton. Marcus was the second son of parents whose principal passion in life had been hunting; they neglected the house. On the top floor, the long gallery had been divided into servants' bedrooms, above which the coved ceiling, covered in a richly swirling pattern of roses, was in a state of collapse. Marcus's mother, Cicely, made no secret of her preference for her dashing first son, Henry, in preference to Marcus, who was short and prematurely bald. 'It was an emotionally hard upbringing,' observes Simon. But Henry died on active service in 1942. Marcus inherited on Cicely's death five years later.

Marcus had been making his own way in life as a land agent and stud manager, for a time working at Highclere. A spell at a stud outside Paris stirred an interest in French art, which he began to collect. On coming into the Burton Agnes estate, he became a successful breeder of racehorses, as well as an astute landowner, with a detailed knowledge of arable farming. Careful management, hard work and an eye for horses enabled him – without the expenses of a family – to keep Burton Agnes staffed and in good repair during the difficult post-War decades. His domestic regime was punctilious. Lunch was at one, tea at five, dinner at eight.

A constant friend was his Spanish assistant, Vicente Arroyo. Part of the year was spent on a large reserve in Kenya which Marcus owned.

The last years of Marcus's life were preoccupied with the search for a suitable heir. A dalliance with the National Trust ended after a senior figure, on a visit of inspection, was overheard to say, 'Of course, the first thing we do when we take over a property like this is to get rid of all the modern art.' Negotiations collapsed. Instead, a preservation trust was created for Burton Agnes Hall and the surrounding land.

Meanwhile, Simon, himself a second son, was growing up on the Swinton estate, on the other side of Yorkshire; Swinton already had an heir in the shape of his brother Mark, Lord Masham. Simon was eight when he knew 'what was coming' as regards Burton Agnes. On Marcus's death, his mother Susan took the reins of the estate, while, after school and Durham University, Simon went to work in London. At Durham he had met Olivia. It was in 2004 that they took a career break and went travelling. On top of a mountain in Peru, they discussed what they would do when they got back. Burton Agnes beckoned. They decided to have a go at it. 'We came because we felt we had energy and years to give which could have been given to employers in London or to investing time in house and community here,' says Simon. 'It meant more to us than increasing share value of large corporations in London.' Now married, they moved into the hall in 2005; Islay, their first child, was born the next year. Burton Agnes now has no live-in staff but can still be 'cranked up' for guests. There is a café in the courtyard, serving the fifty thousand visitors who come to the house each year; it can provide help when needed. 'It has a great chef.' The dining room is pressed into action. The house comes alive.

The hall is not actually where the family live day to day. Most of their time is spent in the Old Rectory, fifty yards away. 'We toyed with moving in as a family to immerse ourselves in living here,' says Olivia. 'We decided to split our time.' Burton Agnes would only be practical if run with a team of staff. 'That's not something we could sustain financially even if we wanted to, and it would make living here quite different from a cosy family home.' The Old Rectory solution is perfect for the time being. The nursery and primary school-aged children are educated in the village, while the eldest three go to fee-paying Pocklington School, on the way to York; they take a bus from nearby Driffield to get there.

The Cunliffe-Listers have set themselves demanding standards in the care of the hall. 'Everything that we do here has to be worthy of the place,' says Olivia. Electrical fittings must be specially made. 'I'm very conscious of the possible encroachment of ugliness. You have to have an eagle eye to stop it, and it's really expensive. We try to make very little impact on the house but do what we must do beautifully. It means a level of control-freakery that is a bit unaccustomed.' All wood – and there is a lot of it – is nurtured. A joiner is employed full time for repairs.

As Simon explains: 'It's the opposite of sweeping something under the carpet. If you decorate a window, you want to make sure everything is properly stripped back. This produces a feeling of satisfaction, even if you don't see what has been done. You know that you're always laying a treasure hunt of wonderful things that will be discovered in years to come. A future owner will say, "Wow, someone's done a really good job. We can do something else now." We are very keen that no harm is done on our watch. Everything we are leaving better than we found it.'

Pins are never knocked into panelling to hang pictures, whatever may have happened in the past. (Picture rails are the way forward.)

Concern for the house also dictates the nature of the commercial activity. 'We have a church. Weddings can take place there, and the house can be hired for celebrations of any kind. But we only host two or three weddings a year. We're disinclined to host weddings that would compromise opening. It's really important to us that the house is open. People can pitch up and be sure it will be open rather than arbitrarily closed. Besides, there's no place to have a disco.' Although big, Burton Agnes is 'reasonably compact.' Holiday accommodation is a better priority. There is a garden fair, an autumn festival and a big Easter egg hunt. The jewel in the crown is a 'really joyous' weekend of jazz, which has a loyal fan base of approaching a thousand festival goers each year. 'It's small but perfectly formed,' says Simon. 'Families come with young children in wellies. Other people set up deckchairs to settle in comfortably. It's a really broad church. It's great.' Part of the inspiration was the family's own music-making, led by Simon on piano and saxophone. 'We're very clear that the activities that take place here are for the benefit of the house.'

One of Burton Agnes's visitors has been David Hockney. 'There was a little flurry of excitement when he came to live in Bridlington. He used to come and paint in the garden.' On one regrettable occasion during the snowdrop opening, he was chased out of the woods by galanthophiles, concerned that he was crushing the flowers. 'We were totally mortified,' says Olivia. 'He can trample as many snowdrops as he wants.'

With five children, how do Simon and Olivia think about succession? The chance will be given in order of seniority, without regard to gender. Number one child has first pick. If she does not want it, the offer will be open to number two; and so on. None of them will have grown up with what Olivia calls an 'ivory tower experience. They see us working very hard, often for other people and broader community. I hope they will feel very little sense of entitlement. We are doing it together as part of a team, with everyone chipping in.' As Simon observes, 'The sense of glamour and grandeur that one perceives from the outside approaching this kind of setup evaporates very quickly when you're plugging away, really. It's not a rarefied existence looking after these geriatric homes.' Admittedly there are some advantages for the younger generation. They have an adventure playground all to themselves, when the paying public have gone home. Birthdays may be celebrated with a Laser Quest party in the woods.

To run Burton Agnes costs around £200,000 a year, not all of which is generated by house opening, café, shop and events. Fortunately the house is at the heart of a three-thousand-acre estate of prime arable land; the family 'chooses to support the trust' with a significant slice of the profits. Why does Simon do it? 'I think it physically encapsulates a personal history and a family history. I'm not big on legacy; I think once you're dead you're done. But we're setting up something to pass onto the next generation. If I reflect on what I've done and what I might have done, the time that I've spent caring for Burton Agnes has been, in extension, caring for something which is important to me: my family.'

Burton Agnes Hall was built in the first decade of the seventeenth century,
by Robert Smythson. Despite an off-centre great hall, care was taken to make the
entrance façade symmetrical: it is entered by a doorway in one of the corner towers.

Previous spread, Music-making is big at Burton Agnes. Events held in the park culminate each year in a 'really joyous' weekend of jazz for families and music lovers of all ages.

This page, The great hall, looking towards the astounding plasterwork of the screen: a treasure trove of Jacobean emblems, religious allegories and unexplained figures. It appears to illustrate the journey of a knight towards the Heavenly City.

The King's State Bedroom. Old panelling, inserted from
elsewhere in the house by Sir Griffith Boynton in the
early eighteenth century, contributes to the poetry of
Burton Agnes. The fragile beauty of wood and textiles
requires constant nurturing by the present owners.

The Queens State Bedroom, with a ceiling of twining honeysuckle. The bed was made for Sowerby House near Bridlington in 1729; it was bought for Burton Agnes in 1934.

The long gallery, which runs across the full width of the house, was restored in the 1950s and 1970s. It now contains a collection of modern sculpture, furniture and ceramics, as well as French paintings.

Some of the French paintings and decorative arts bought by Marcus Wickham-Boynton in the mid twentieth century. He decided against giving Burton Agnes to the National Trust when a senior figure was overheard to say, 'Of course, the first thing we do when we take over a property like this is to get rid of all the modern art.'

Looking back from the long gallery towards the gatehouse; beyond it is the fertile plain of Holderness. When Celia Fiennes visited in the late seventeenth century, there was a bowling green. Bobble-shaped yew topiaries now delineate the lawns and paths.

Previous spread, London Transport Routemaster bus, 1960: a wedding present from Olivia's mother, Liz Bolton, to Olivia and Simon.

This Page, Otis enjoying the woodland adventure playground.

Opposite, Islay, Olivia, Simon, Inigo, Otis and Sholto in the walled garden's potager.

THE HISTORY OF
BURTON AGNES HALL

Next to the hall at Burton Agnes is a small brick-faced building, containing the vaults and first-floor hall of a Norman manor house. Built around 1180, probably by Sir Roger de Stuteville, the house has never been sold since.

Within sight of the sea, on a broad agricultural plain in the East Riding of Yorkshire, the estate was inherited, in 1574, by fifteen-year old Sir Henry Griffith. To begin with, Sir Henry must have lived in Staffordshire, where he was High Sheriff and a Justice of the Peace. But he was appointed to the Council of the North in 1599, and this inspired him to rebuild Burton Agnes, which has the date 1601 on the panel above the front door and 1610 in a frieze in a bedroom. The investment paid off, since during that decade he was knighted and made High Sheriff of Yorkshire. Sir Henry's architect was no doubt Robert Smythson, since a ground plan (not as built) exists in the Royal Institute of British Architects' Drawings Collection.

The setting of the house, with its gatehouse, is still recognisably Jacobean, although the bowling green is now a lawn scattered with bobble-like yew hedges. Beyond the lawn, the house rises in a series of bays and gables built of rosy orange brick, silvered with lichen. There are two square and two semi-circular bays; the square bays are surmounted by strapwork crests. This is an ordered composition, full of the tall transom windows that had been fashionable since the cheaper availability of glass in the second half of the sixteenth century. It is also sophisticated in its bid for symmetry. In earlier houses, the dominance of the great hall, entered from the 'low' end by a screens passage, forced the entrance door to be placed off centre. Smythson overcame this by balancing the bay to the great hall (on the right) by another containing a doorway (on the left). However, the doorway cannot be seen, since it has been turned at right angles to the façade. Despite the inconspicuous position, the entrance is dignified with a treatment of superimposed orders (Ionic, Corinthian, Composite, but no Doric) and a carving of Sir Henry's coat of arms.

Visitors using this entrance then enter a screens passage and turn right into the great hall. Opposite the entrance is a monumental doorway carved with vines and Renaissance motifs, including four figures from Mount Olympus. Naked and rather skinny in comparison to usual depictions of gods and goddesses, they are identified by scrolls: Saturn (devouring a child) and Jupiter (with eagle) on the left, Mars (with helmet, buckler and sword) and Venus (scantly draped) on the right. Their divine status is signified by suns bursting behind their heads. After this display of Classical erudition, it is something of a surprise to turn around and see the decoration of the screen. Although the wooden lower part has round-headed arches separated by pairs of Ionic columns, the tiers of plasterwork – hampers as they are technically called – is something of a riot of emblems, allegories and religious iconography. Seven female figures at the top must represent the Heavenly Virtues. Below them, in the top hamper, is a scene which appears to show a Christian knight being led into the Heavenly City by angels. The knight is surely Sir Henry Griffith. In the lowest hamper are the Evangelists, identified by their symbols. The panels between them and the spaces to either side contain seven figures, whom it would be tempting to call the Seven Deadly Sins; however, their attributes are hardly obvious.

The carvings on the screen itself are easier to decipher, having been labelled by the artist; they include the twelve tribes of Israel, the twelve apostles and, in the keystones to the arches, the Sybils who predicted the birth of Christ. While the frame in which all these wooden and plaster characters stand is Classical, the impression is as much one of profusion – and, to the uninitiated spectator, puzzlement – as a medieval stained-glass window.

As Pevsner and Neave's *The Buildings of England* volume on the East Riding comments, here is 'the most crazily overcrowded screen in all England,' but it is 'one of the glories of Burton Agnes.'

The iconography of the alabaster relief above the fireplace can be determined without assistance; it shows the Five Wise and Five Foolish Virgins, all of whom receive their just deserts at the Last Trump. Above this sits a magnificent carved wooden section brought from another family house in the East Riding, Barmston Hall, in the 1760s. The staircase is a dramatic piece of open carpentry, rising tightly around a structure supported on tall arches, its surfaces sumptuously carved with a pattern of guilloche (interlaced ribbons).

At the top of the house, the long gallery runs across the whole width of the entrance front. To either end are Palladian windows introduced during the eighteenth century. The plaster ceiling swirls with the stems and flowers of roses: a careful replica of the original, much of which had collapsed in 1810 due to a leaking roof. The restoration was conducted in two campaigns in the 1950s and 1970s, under the expert eye of the architect Francis Johnson. Elsewhere, Burton Agnes contains not only its original plasterwork but panelling and portraits of the period, as well as beds and other furniture from the eighteenth century. Impressionist and Modern British paintings collected by Marcus Wickham-Boynton in the mid twentieth century and late twentieth century furniture by John Makepeace show that the house, however fragile, continues to evolve.

HUTTON-IN-THE-FOREST

Cumbria

Cressida, Lady Inglewood and Thisbe, one of her two lurchers, on the terrace at Hutton-in-the-Forest:
she finds the colour of the stone particularly pleasing.

I am sitting on the terrace of Hutton-in-the-Forest, an ancient country house in Cumbria; it is autumn and the sun casts a golden light over the landscape before us, where a tractor has trundled onto the scene to remove some hay bales. Old cedars cast long shadows. A seventeenth-century garden may be hidden in the woods beyond the stream. Richard, 2nd Baron Inglewood, Hutton-in-the-Forest's owner, thinks so, and will, I suspect, have proved it before long. As a lawyer he is used to proving things, as well as posing difficult questions. It was Richard who asked the questions that started this book: what is the point of country houses today? What do they mean? It is now his turn to answer. Although on a day like this, they practically answer themselves.

Richard has no hesitation in replying: 'I see Hutton as an installation, like a piece of modern sculpture. You've got the house, the contents, the grounds – they all relate to each other. They are a work of art. From a wider perspective, if I'm right, they have a value which is completely separate from what they mean to me. There would be a loss to the country if they went to the four winds.'

In its out of the way location, between Penrith and Carlisle, Hutton-in-the-Forest is not hugely visited; nevertheless, between ten thousand and fifteen thousand people either go round it, or attend events held there each year. 'If you look at our visitors' book, some of them have clearly enjoyed the experience.' Visiting country houses is a well-established pastime, familiar since the late seventeenth century. Nowadays, it offers a different experience from the State-subsidised generality of British arts. For a country house in private ownership is not the same as an art gallery or museum; part of the meaning of each work of art or piece of furniture derives from its proximity to all the other contents of the house.

Contents have a value as an ensemble which they might not have individually. Besides, they're enjoyable to see. 'If you want to attract people into areas like this, which need investment, you must have things that interest and amuse them. Country houses should be part of the mix.'

Richard's wife, Cressida, a photographer turned gardener, looks at Hutton-in-the-Forest in a different light. 'I don't feel that purpose is important. I think Hutton a very beautiful house, its pale pink-grey sandstone is a wonderful back drop to the garden and it sits very happily in the landscape. I like the fact that every generation has added to and altered parts of the house. We in our turn had a year of building works, demolished a tower of loos, swapped around an entrance and a staircase, moved fireplaces and doorways and so on.'

Richard grew up at Hutton-in-the-Forest. It has not been absolutely convenient to his career. The ten years during which he served as a Member of the European Parliament meant a weekly dash to Brussels (via Newcastle) or Strasbourg (via Manchester and Zurich). He is still a politician, sitting on the Conservative benches in the House of Lords. 'If you're ambitious for high office, it would be impossible to pursue your goal from Hutton. We're not so big we can have hired hands doing everything; we have to run the show ourselves. Although Cressida does much more of the dogsbody work than I do.'

For Cressida, the commitment to Hutton-in-the-Forest came with her marriage in 1986. Fortunately, she had also been brought up in a Cumbrian country house and so knew what she was taking on. But it was a far cry from her previous existence in London where she had a successful career as a photographer.

'What I liked was photographing landscapes and gardens, mostly for books and magazines, although I did portraits as well. I did one book after we got married – *Beatrix Potter's Lakeland*, then house and children and digital photography took over'.

Having come from an under-resourced, over-sized house, Cressida was not daunted by Hutton-in-the- Forest. It was in fair condition but unimaginatively decorated. 'After the war, Richard's parents did what they could. They demolished a billiard room and Victorian back premises, they put in bathrooms, some with avocado suites which were fashionable at the time. There had been little electricity before they arrived and they didn't use the front of the house much, probably for one drinks party at Christmas each year. It gets much more use now. I married into a bachelor household - Richard, his father, and at weekends his brother, along with a cook and three dailies. I clung on to the cook until about four years ago. We have a caretaker, and daily help is now down to four mornings a week, with cooking on Fridays and occasional weekends.' She accepts that life at Hutton-in-the-Forest imposes certain conditions - such as the need to travel to see friends. 'Up here you're used to going twenty miles for tea. The other day we went to lunch in Northumberland, over one hundred miles each way.' She loves the garden and would not work nearly as hard at it if it were not for the visitors. 'We don't have many unusual plants; everything has got to be happy and thrive in quite tough conditions. For me what is important is the visual joy.'

Beyond the garden wall is the community that surrounds Hutton-in-the-Forest. It barely has a village; the little church on the edge of the park, where Richard is Church Warden (and, without a vicar for the moment, sometimes leads services), would lose a pillar of support if it were not for the big house. 'We employ people,' he says. 'We do business with people in Penrith. I have chaired local companies and represented the area as an MEP. I chair the Local Enterprise Partnership. Events are held here. There is a food fair, a classic car show and the yearly Potfest, believed to be the biggest pottery festival in the UK'. The Inglewoods are themselves buyers, as can be seen from the contemporary ceramics around the house. 'The house is the backdrop to these events. It provides a focus and context which enhances the experience.' Part of the charm of the Hutton-in-the-Forest events is their small scale. This is not entirely a matter of choice, although Richard is alive to the danger of overexploiting the house and wrecking its character as a work of art. It is simply in the wrong place. 'If you have big local population you can do well. That is not our position.'

Some events may be more enjoyable than others for the owners of Hutton-in-the-Forest but all involve work. 'The idea of a place like this producing "unearned income" is nonsense. They are businesses; they may not be very profitable businesses but if you don't approach them in a hard-headed way, they will go to Carey Street. They weren't built as private residences. They were places to show off, exert political power, and be a corporate headquarters.' This need not be incompatible with beauty. 'Motives can be mixed. At Houghton, Sir Robert Walpole wanted to build a magnificent palace which gave him pleasure; but also to overwhelm his neighbours and have them in the palm of his hand.' A country house, though, is not a conventional business, for the obvious reason that – however unpromising its location – it must stay put. 'If I were making widgets, I'd move my factory. I can't do that with Hutton.'

Country houses were, when first created, expensive to build; now they are expensive to keep going. 'It's pouring money into a bucket with a hole in it. Roofs leak. Drains gets blocked. Electrical aspects must be kept up to date; if you don't do that you can't get insurance. Visitors produce wear and tear; you must employ staff to put that right. So you have to accept that building is never going to pay its way on its own terms. As I say to my son, "You either have to get a job that will pay for it or find a way of endowing it".' The house has a maintenance fund: a mechanism by which capital dedicated specially to the restoration of the property can be preserved from tax. Richard set it up when his father died in 1989, under a different tax regime from now. 'The rules later changed, but it was the right thing to do at the time, to keep the show on the road for another generation.' Hutton-in-the-Forest is not currently in trust. 'For the time being, it is my personal property subject to undertakings I've given to the Treasury to look after it properly and the wider laws of the land. The problem with trusts is that they can box you in.'

There are people who live comfortably with gambling – call them entrepreneurs. Richard is not among their number. He is not a Quaker but once chaired a Quaker company and found the approach sympathetic. 'I think it is possible to make money from this place but I don't feel I should. It's not the right way to treat things, since it would be spoiled, if not ruined.' A boon for many country houses, Hutton included, is the boom in art prices. A theoretical boon. 'Assets have gone up in value since the 1970s. But if you start plundering the works of art they aren't here anymore. Country houses have been called the National Gallery of the regions. I've tried very hard not to sell anything of quality because otherwise, if everyone did it, Cumbria won't have anything of quality. Unfortunately, the cost of repairs and employing people has gone up hugely, along with works of art; specialist building works are not cheap. It's good fun to have houses like this, but I wouldn't go and buy one.'

And the world can change. 'If a government comes in that wants to nationalise land and impose wealth tax, the party's over. You need to think of these things and ponder the future.'

It is too early to envisage a transition to the next generation. As Richard tells his three offspring, he is not King Lear, who divided his kingdom between a trio of daughters to disastrous effect. When the time comes, Hutton will descend, as it always has, by primogeniture. 'I told Henry to go away and make as much money as he can. I hope he will. He's twenty-nine, and that's far too early for him to live somewhere like here. I want him to be at least forty. I came back at thirty because my father wasn't very well and my mother soon died; but I regret it. What do they know of England who only England know? You have to get out there and know the world is full of sharks and shysters. You have to have a hard-nosed edge. But this is a place that draws people back.'

Handing over would mean moving on. Where would Cressida make a new home? 'I truly don't know; I want one big living space with light and a view. Space must be the greatest luxury. A warm cottage with low ceilings and small windows doesn't appeal. Besides, Richard has his books - he keeps coming back from the Charing Cross Road laden with new volumes. I cannot see him going out except feet first. Henry rightly says that we have too much 'stuff', I expect he'll throw a lot out when he gets the chance.'

But that is for a distant future. For now the hay has been cut, the sun shines and it is very nearly time for a drink.

Hutton-in-the-Forest was made 'regular' in the late seventeenth century, when the Classical frontispiece was added; it was romantically unbalanced in the Victorian period, when the architect Salvin, aided by George Webster of Kendal, added the south-east tower.

Previous spread, Cressida Inglewood on the battlements. One of the projects of recent years has been to open up views in the park, which had become overgrown. The pond is one of three, fed by the beck and originally stocked with fish for the table.

This page, The early nineteenth century Main Stairs rise up the full height of the house. They were introduced at the same time as the Gothic south-east tower was built, part of the changes carried out by Sir Francis Fletcher-Vane.

The Regency drawing
room, overlaid with
Victorian decoration in
Aesthetic taste.

This page & opposite, Lady Darlington's Room,
named after Caroline Vane, Countess of Darlington
who was a cousin of the family and a regular visitor.
It was decorated with William Morris wallpaper
by Lady Vane in the late nineteenth century.

Richard and Cressida Inglewood in the staircase hall. The Cupid stair, with its boldly carved balustrade of winged boys swinging on acanthus leaves, was moved from another part of the house in the nineteenth century. 'Hutton is a romantic place,' says Richard.

Opposite, Pele tower and open loggia. Above the latter is the long gallery: built in the 1630s. It is a deliberately backward-looking style, which recalls the architectural works of Lady Anne Clifford, a neighbour.

This page, The pele tower now forms the entrance to the house.

Opposite, A bay off the long gallery, with one of the many pieces of contemporary ceramics in the house. Every year Hutton-in-the-Forest hosts a festival of ceramics – Potfest in the Park.

Left, Lily of the valley gates made by Scottish artist-blacksmith Adam Booth.

Right, The date stone over the door, 1988, commemorates the work Cressida and Richard did on the house when they moved in in the second half of the 1980's.

Left, Ministerial red boxes.

Right, A view across the
dining table into the kitchen.

Opposite, Thisbe, the lurcher,
in hope. No country kitchen is
complete without a dog.

THE HISTORY OF
HUTTON-IN-THE-FOREST

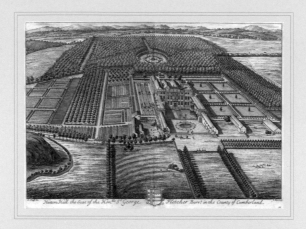

Hutton-in-the-Forest is a name that evokes the wilderness that was Cumberland in the Middle Ages. Yet the surroundings of the house today are not so fearsome, and the grounds contain the traces of past gardens, as well as plentiful evidence of much gardening in the present generation.

In about 1670, Daniel Fleming of Rydal, brother-in-law of the then owner Sir George Fletcher, described Hutton-in-the-Forest as having been 'formerly a strong place having a high tower well moated about with a drawbridge over it which was a good defence against the Scottish inroads.' By then, however, the original family – the Huttons, who took their name from the place – had sold it, in 1606, to Richard Fletcher of Cockermouth. Fletcher probably enlarged it to the west. Richard's son, Henry, was made a baronet in 1641. Soon he was building at Hutton, adding the long gallery in a retardataire style; the first-floor bay projects over an open loggia and is supported on clustered columns of cathedral type.

During the Civil War, Sir Henry tried to hold Carlisle for the King, but was defeated by the Parliament-supporting Scottish army. Sir Henry died fighting at a skirmish in Cheshire, while his widow and son, the young Sir George, were imprisoned in Carlisle Castle. Having compounded for her estates, Lady Fletcher was careful not to invite further penalty; when the young Charles II came south on his way to the Battle of Worcester in 1651, she did not invite him into the house but had food sent out to the gates of the park. The pace of building picked up again after the Restoration but to a different plan. By this time, Sir George had put detention in Carlisle Castle behind him, having become, according to a description of 1675, 'a very brave monsr.'.

It was Sir George who added the Classical centrepiece to the entrance front, not only in a different style and on a different scale to the towers to either side, but in stone of a different colour. The cream of the new work contrasts with the pink of the local stone. Rubbing shoulders to right and left, the highly architectural if rather crowded façade has the appearance of a smart terraced house in Mayfair, which has been magically transported to this Border location. The architect/builder was the Westmorland mason Edward Addison, who had worked at Lowther Hall. The clergyman and antiquary Thomas Machell claimed that he and Addison were 'the first introducers of Regular building into these Parts.'

Sir George's son Henry had little interest in the house, which, according to Bishop Nicolson who visited in 1705, was 'over-run with Rats, wch eat all his Beds [and] Hangings.' But he was a plantsman, interested in new discoveries from 'ye Indies', who kept 'the gardens in very good condition.' A difficult character, he became a Roman Catholic, sold most of his property and became associated with a religious order in Douai, in Flanders. His death there was followed by a long suit in Chancery.

In the 1720s, Hutton passed to the Vanes, who sometimes called themselves Fletcher-Vane. From 1735-59, Henry Vane-Fletcher (his mother was one of Sir George's Fletcher's daughters) planted avenues, made ponds in the park and commissioned the delightful plasterwork of the Cupid Room on the first floor of the pele tower. A charming image of the time is provided by William Hogarth's conversation piece of Henry's younger brother *Walter Vane and his Family*. They sit around a table in a garden, Mrs Vane dandling an infant girl on her knee as the son and heir, Lionel, comes forward with a dove in his hands. This was not, however, painted at Hutton, which Walter did not inherit until long afterwards.

The last major campaign of work at Hutton began around 1826, when Sir Francis Fletcher-Vane's architect was Anthony Salvin. Work, which included construction of the South-East tower with George Webster of Kendal, continued for several decades – indeed it was not finished until the end of the century, many years after Salvin's death in 1881. This may reflect a restricted budget, since the Fletcher-Vanes' finances, never princely, were reduced by an expensive legal action brought by Sir Francis's brother, Frederick, against Sir Francis's son, Sir Henry, claiming that the latter had been born out of wedlock. By 1900, the vaulted base of the pele tower had been turned into a new entrance and the big tower to the south-east had been refaced. Sir Henry's wife, Margaret Gladstone, a cousin of the former Liberal Prime Minister, took an active interest in the Arts and Crafts movement and the surviving William Morris wallpapers are part of her contribution to the house.

After her death in 1915, Hutton eventually passed to a distant cousin, William Vane, created 1st Lord Inglewood. He, his wife and the trustees stabilised the finances and adapted the house and estate for a new era; some nineteenth-century additions to the house were demolished. His elder son Richard, 2nd Lord Inglewood, and his wife Cressida have adjusted the house further, decorating it with the contemporary ceramics and hand-printed textiles seen in the photographs.

DODDINGTON HALL

Lincolnshire

Claire and James Birch at Doddington Hall, Lincolnshire, beneath stags' heads.
The style of Claire's parents, who used to live here, was more minimalist.

Doddington Hall in Lincolnshire is one of those country houses you find only in Britain. The attics are full of old toys, military headgear, unwanted commodes and a giant figure of the White Rabbit, left over from an Alice in Wonderland-themed event. Tapestries are used like wallpaper and there are so many of them that the house has its own studio for textile repairs. A collection of Roman antiquities, some found on the estate, is displayed in the downstairs lavatory, along with a child's pedal-operated aeroplane with patriotic RAF roundels. From the roof, you can see Lincoln cathedral on a good day. Built around 1600, Doddington has hardly been changed outside, and in half a millennium, it has never been sold.

Today's owners, James and Claire Birch, came in 2007 after busy working lives that had taken them to Hong Kong and India. James worked in the City, Claire in advertising – so rural Lincolnshire was about as far from their previous habitats as the moon. 'What I love about it is the luxury of having a vegetable garden. It gives me huge satisfaction that everything we eat or serve to guests is produced from the estate, including beef and venison.' For her, London now belongs to a different, distant phase of existence. 'I don't miss it but crazily enough it sometimes feels as though it would be a bit more peaceful there.' What with cleaners, electricians, guides, delivery drivers, conservators and all the other people who contribute to the running of a country house – not to mention the visiting public – 'lack of privacy is a big issue. I can't even dream of spending the morning in a dressing gown, reading magazines – although that's probably a fantasy anyway.'

Before their arrival, the Hall had been home to Claire's father Antony Jarvis, who had farmed the 2,000-acre estate. He had not quite grown up in the Hall: the family only came at weekends when he was a boy. Apart from open fires, Doddington's main source of warmth was many paraffin heaters: it was Antony's job as a lad to keep them topped up. Tin bathtubs were positioned to catch leaks from the roof. These were the post-Second World War years: a difficult time for country houses. Antony's father had worked in a merchant bank, but a director's salary was not what it became after the liberalisation of the City of London with Big Bang in the 1980s.

But in the mid-1970s, Antony and his wife Victoria made the brave decision that Doddington should be their main home. Previously, Antony had spent nine happy years at Cambridge University, reading natural sciences, land economy and architecture. Architecture, which he studied for five years, did not in the end look as though it would provide a worthwhile career, and he never pursued the final qualification (it would have taken another two years). Agriculture, however, was doing well; farmers were being encouraged to become more efficient, with the help of government and European subsidies. Taxes, on the other hand, were swingeing. It was a tax exemption offered to owners of Grade I listed houses whose farmland constituted part of the historic setting that encouraged him to plant an Avenue Walk. This in turn demanded a folly to stop the view. Antony had already designed a Temple of the Winds, dedicated to his parents, in the Wild Garden: the dome of it he built himself out of fibreglass. He longed now for an eyecatcher that would terminate the avenue. He had many years to wait before his wish would be fulfilled.

For the Hall needed urgent attention. An outbreak of deathwatch beetle had reduced the ends of the tie beam that held the outside walls together, to a powder resembling snuff.

Wind whistled between the lights of the Elizabethan windows whose iron muntins had rusted. Fortunately, Antony and Victoria made a favourable impression on the newly established Historic Buildings Council, which visited with its chairman Dame Jennifer Jenkins; in those far off days, they were given an eighty per cent grant for repairs. They were also given listed buildings consent to regularise the fenestration on the garden front, the Georgians having lowered some but not all of the windows. The house was redecorated in the spare style of the time – no clutter.

With three daughters but no sons, Antony and Victoria were faced with a dilemma over the future of Doddington. Who would live there? The problem to some extent solved itself: one of Claire's sisters lives in Finland, the other in France. Of the three, Claire was the one most interested in the house – although a question remained as to how a sufficient income could be generated to run it. Antony did not find it a wrench to leave the big house; the elegantly converted Game House provides a much more convenient home. Sadly, Victoria had little time to enjoy it: she died of cancer in 2006.

Antony's interest has always been in the garden, which he continues to run. Having planted bulbs in the wild garden since he inherited the house, he can now enjoy the clumps of white, mauve and magenta – snowdrop, crocus and cyclamen – which sparkle like jewels among the grass of early spring. Previous plantings of daffodils had formed what he calls a 'Russian salad' of different varieties: 'some were hideous – great big modern ones which I've extirpated. The interesting ones I have separated and spread.'

It was in 2014 that Antony's dream of a folly for the avenue came true: he persuaded James and Claire, now running the estate, to build a pyramid.

The blocks come from the concrete floor of a grain store, broken up by a mechanical pecker. This provides a rusticated effect, with the blocks diminishing in size towards the top. Quartzite pebbles in the concrete make it glitter in the sunshine.

James and Claire were lucky. Adapting the house for a family with three (then) teenage children was relatively easy. 'These days, people want kitchens at the front of the house, overlooking the gardens and possibly the drive,' says James, who, as chairman of the Historic Houses Association, knows what other private owners are doing. 'Our kitchen had already been moved. We don't have a large central hall, which gives you nowhere to hide when the public come round. Doddington is long and thin. We live at one end, in about a quarter of it.' On high days and holidays, the whole of the house is pressed into use.

The best innovation, according to Claire, has been a woodchip heating system. 'It meant we had to lose the Aga which used oil. I'd thought a house without an Aga couldn't be home. But we put extra radiators into the kitchen and got an induction hob – it's fantastic.' Claire and James also revamped their shared office. 'The old Victorian furniture didn't work with computers. We had new desks made from salvaged teak. It's now the warmest room in the house and I have to be careful not to stay there till midnight.' Textiles collected in the Far East have been hung in a bedroom, which also contains a collection of 'bad taste Cultural Revolution memorabilia.' The library, where the floor had to be replaced when it was found that the Elizabethan joists had rotted through after having been placed directly on soil, has been repainted in blue-black Farrow & Ball 'Railings'. 'It used to have very bright Linen Union curtains from the 1970s. They'd become very faded.'

So Claire personally stitched on new linen panels 'and we should get another hundred years of use out of them.' Far from banishing all clutter, James has a yen for salerooms, acquisitions from which enrich the texture of the house.

How to keep Doddington going? It first opened to the public in 1954: to do so, for one day a week in those days, was a requirement of grants. Now, thirty thousand visitors come around Doddington each year; after the closure each autumn, it opens again for the month before Christmas, five days a week. But opening the house makes little more than a small dent in the cost of running it. Over the last decade, to bolster the modest income from visitors, James and Claire have redeveloped the derelict home farm buildings, close enough to the Hall to be associated with it, but also on a busy road. The first venture, a farm shop, was originally just an outlet for the kitchen garden. This has now expanded twice and sells lots of Lincolnshire products including Doddington vegetables, beef from the estate herd of Lincoln Red cattle and honey from hives on the farm. Beyond the farm shop are a busy café and a slightly more formal restaurant. Later retail additions have been a homewares store, a country clothing store and a huge bicycle shop with its own cyclists' coffee shop. These operations run almost every day of the year, and the combination of growing and selling Christmas trees and decorations, mean that November and December have become the most important trading months of the year for Doddington.

Like many historic houses Doddington is host to numerous weddings and events. Civil ceremonies are possible in the long gallery, but the fabric of the Hall is deemed too fragile for much else, so all the eating and drinking takes place in a purpose-built events venue.

Nobody gets to stay in the house, but a series of holiday cottages allow up to fifty people to overnight on site. All of these new enterprises are run by the estate and employ almost a hundred people, probably more than worked on the estate at its agricultural peak.

Country house owners must seize – or make – new opportunities. 'A lot of places have been kept afloat by the reasonably benign environment for agriculture created by the European Union. This may not continue.' Similarly, a recent survey showed that one in six country houses have been selling works of art or furniture to fund repairs. Will the art market remain strong? 'The two biggest asset classes associated with country houses may not be so good in the future,' says James. 'Meanwhile, the cost of repairs doesn't get any less, while visitor expectations rise all the time. The National Trust is about to spend £100m on improving its shops and cafes. That's not so easy for the private sector.' On the other hand, Doddington has something that the properties of the National Trust do not have. It is a true family home.

This page, Antony Jarvis and the pyramid that he designed for the park. It is built out of concrete blocks quarried from a redundant grain store and roughly shaped. Quartzite pebbles in the concrete make it sparkle.

Next spread, Doddington Hall was completed in 1600: the symmetry of the composition suggest that it was designed by Robert Smythson, also the likely architect of Burton Agnes Hall. From the roof it is possible to see Lincoln cathedral, where the client, Thomas Taylor, was the Bishop's Registrar or Recorder.

Tapestries and treasures at Doddington. The tapestries, used as wall-hangings in some rooms, are an exceptional survival; many were placed in position as part of a backward-looking decorative scheme in the mid-eighteenth century. These show the Pensive Unicorn and *(opposite, bottom right)* a bagpiper and dog.

A downstairs lavatory, *(opposite, bottom left)*, contains a display case showing Roman and other antiquities, some of them found in the park. The serried rank of boots bears witness to the importance of outdoor life, *(opposite, top right)*.

The mirror, (*top left*), with its gilt frame carved with putti, cherubs' heads, fruit and flowers is believed to come from the future James II's yacht. In 1671, it was given to Captain Christopher Gunman, who commanded the yacht, when the Duke of York, as he then was, ordered new furniture. One of Gunman's descendants inherited Doddington.

The Great Stair with its shallow treads was erected by Sir John Hussey-Delaval in the mid-eighteenth century.

James Birch. James, who is President of the Historic Houses Association, converted the stables at Doddington to house several shops and a restaurant; the house is visited by thirty thousand people each year, the stables by quarter of a million.

Previous spread, The original Elizabethan great hall was redecorated in 1763 in slightly old-fashioned style. The bobbin chairs are Cromwellian but the table was made from estate oak in the 1990's. On the far right of the mantelpiece is the gibbeting iron that held Tom Otter, hanged in 1806 for the murder of his bigamous second wife.

This page, The library book shelves were brought to Doddington from Dover Castle where George Jarvis was Governor in the 1820s. The 2003 painting of James, Claire, George, Luke and Alice is by Julika De Fouw.

Foremost amongst the paintings in the long gallery is Joshua Reynold's *The Earl and Countess of Mexborough with their son, Lord Pollington* on their way to the Coronation of George III. Sarah Mexborough was the youngest and most beautiful of the five Delaval daughters.

This page & opposite, Despite having lived in Hong Kong, India and London before coming to Doddington, Claire took to Lincolnshire without difficulty. 'What I love about it is the luxury of having a vegetable garden. It gives me huge satisfaction that everything we eat or serve to guests is produced from the estate, including beef and venison.'

Antony Jarvis's interest has always been in the garden, which he continues to run. Having been planting bulbs in the wild garden since he inherited the house, he can now enjoy the clumps of white, mauve and magenta – snowdrop, crocus and cyclamen – which sparkle like jewels among the grass of early spring. Previous plantings of daffodils had formed what he calls a 'Russian salad' of different varieties: 'some were hideous – great big modern ones which I've extirpated. The interesting ones I have separated and spread.'

THE HISTORY OF DODDINGTON HALL

Doddington was built in the last decade of the sixteenth century: the date of completion was 1600, recorded on a lead plate on top of the central cupola. The architect was almost certainly Robert Smythson, who designed Wollaton Hall in Nottinghamshire and Hardwick Hall in Derbyshire. It is significant that Lincoln Cathedral can be seen from the roof because Smythson's client, Thomas Taylor, was the Bishop's Registrar or Recorder: no doubt the office provided some of the money that built Doddington. This is one of the first houses to have a straight parapet, hiding the roof, rather than Elizabethan gables. The idea of the three cupolas above the parapet was probably borrowed from Burleigh, the great Lincolnshire house outside Stamford, finished in the 1580s.

The clay for Doddington's red bricks was dug from an adjoining field, now a meadow in the garden, and burnt on site. The limestone for quoins and window dressings was to be had from the Lincoln Cliff ridge. Planned as an H, with bays in the corners, the result is a rather

severe house; the Renaissance doorcase in the centre of the entrance front is one of few enrichments. Banks of mullion windows, still containing their old glass, glitter in the sunshine.

Taylor was not succeeded by a dynasty of squires bearing his name, since his son died childless. Indeed, surnames of owners have constantly changed throughout the history of the house. But from the day that it was built, Doddington has never been sold. Taylor's daughter herself had a daughter, who married into the Hussey family. From the Husseys it passed, again by marriage, to the Delavals of Seaton Delaval in Northumberland.

For Doddington, the most important of this line was John Hussey Delaval, who inherited the house, as a second son, in 1759. In time, he would also own the other family properties of Seaton Delaval and Ford Castle in Northumberland, doing work to them all. His campaign at Doddington began in 1760. However, he did not employ a fashionable architect, relying instead on William Portis, a joiner from Scotland. Sir John, as he became in 1761, preferred the old-fashioned style of the interiors he had known from his childhood, with sometimes a glance further back. Rooms such as the hall were Georgianised, but with fireplaces and doorcases of a more robust style than one would expect of the date. Some of the bedrooms were close hung with tapestries in the manner of William and Mary's age. In 1762, Portis reported that he had had 'a tayler all this week mending the tapestry before we hung it up.' The chimneypiece of the Holly Room was given a Gothic frieze.

This scheme of decoration, remarkable in itself as an example of conservative taste, caused some unusual tapestries to be conserved. Though beautiful and delightful – the country figures depicted include a bagpiper and a sportsman resting with his gun – they are rare because of their second tier status; because elsewhere, more care has been taken to preserve only the finest tapestries, many of which are now in museums or owned by the National Trust, than less exalted works such as these.

On his death, at the age of eighty-five in 1808, Sir John was buried in Westminster Abbey. Alas, his only son – another John – had already died of consumption shortly before his 21st birthday. The beer brewed for the party that would have celebrated his coming of age stayed in the cellar; it is still there, never opened. So the house passed first to his brother, Edward, and then to Edward's daughter, Sarah. Aged thirty-three, Sarah married Admiral James Gunman of Dover in 1805. In Dover, she became well known both for her philanthropy and soirées, the latter being attended by a handsome officer, Lieutenant-Colonel George Jarvis. Gunman died in 1824 and his widow would have married Jarvis, only she too was carried away by consumption. As a testament to her love, she left Doddington to her fiancé.

The print room is now lined with the drawings that Jarvis made on his travels. He was not only a talented artist but a skilled wood carver too; a cabinet contains his large collection of chisels.

But Jarvis and his successors did little to change the Georgian interiors that they inherited, or the Elizabethan shell in which they are encased. As John Cornforth wrote in *Country Life* (February 3, 1994), the effect is 'remarkably felicitous.'

A further word must be said about the pyramid, already mentioned, completed in 2014. It is the work of the Antony Jarvis, father of Claire Birch who now lives with her family in the main house. Before he began to farm the estate in the 1970s, Antony had spent nine happy years at Cambridge University, reading natural sciences, land economy and architecture. Architecture, which he studied for five years, did not in the end look as though it would provide a worthwhile career, and he never pursued the final qualification. Nevertheless it equipped him to undertake this folly, having previously designed a Temple of the Winds, dedicated to his parents, in the Wild Garden: the dome of it he built himself out of fibreglass.

As previously described, the building material came from the floor of a redundant grain store. While most pyramids in English landscape parks are angled at 45 degrees, Antony chose a steeper pitch for the sides – 70 degrees. This gives it a somewhat French look, like the pyramid in the Parc Monceau. It also allowed for a door, which gives into a saucer-domed vault, where already water dripping through the concrete has created stalactites and stalagmites. Altogether the pyramid looks as though it might have been there for centuries.

BROUGHTON CASTLE

Oxfordshire

The Hon. Martin and Pauline Fiennes, with sons Ned, Ivo and Guy, in the kitchen at Broughton Castle, installed in the 1970s beneath a fourteenth-century vault.

Martin Fiennes is a busy man. Last week he took down 'all the pictures and moved all the furniture' at Broughton Castle, with a team that included two conservators and three local builders, who erected scaffold towers. Today, a man from the Pitt-Rivers Museum in Oxford is coming to research a canoe, said to have been brought back from Hawaii by Captain Cook – although, as the man points out, Captain Cook himself did not return from Hawaii (the canoe was sold from the Castle in 1837). On my previous visit, Martin was occupied with a hornets' nest which had appeared in one of the lavatories. Dylan, the photographer, came the day after youngest son Ivo's eighteenth birthday party, during which a breastplate from the English Civil War – one of seven – temporarily went missing, to be found next to the deep freeze. Nothing daunts him. He loves it all. Broughton Castle has been here since the fourteenth century and, when Martin inherits the family's title, created in 1447, he will be the 22nd Baron Saye and Sele. Despite all the weight of tradition, he declares that 'change is fun.'

The zest with which Martin enjoys Broughton is infectious. It is as though the castle is an endlessly fascinating toy box. We are in the great hall when I suggest that he must work very hard to keep the place going. 'Just self-indulgence,' he says with a smile. 'It's a lovely thing to do. It's a lovely place to be. You could write a list of fifty different things that could become areas of interest or hobbies.' He gestures to a pair of sofas, upholstered at the turn of the twentieth century in crimson plush, made in the nearby village of Shutford. 'Wouldn't it be great to learn about the plush industry in nineteenth-century Oxfordshire.' He looks around the room. 'I'd love to know about sixteenth-century furniture or medieval armour. You could be interested in Tudor wall hangings, or lime plaster ceilings, or Sanderson Miller, who lived nearby and probably designed

this ceiling in the eighteenth century. The list goes on. That's an incredible privilege – all that pleasure. There's a bit of duty that comes into it. My parents did an amazing job here. You have a duty to that, too, as well as to the place itself.'

Over the fireplace is a portrait of William of Wykeham, the great Bishop of Winchester and Chancellor of the Exchequer who founded Winchester College and New College, Oxford, and oversaw Edward III's development of Windsor Castle, as well as effectively running the government of the land. He bought Broughton in 1377 and gave it to his sister's grandson. It has been in that family ever since. 'A Fiennes married a Wykeham heiress. In the seventeenth century, a daughter who was Baroness Saye and Sele in her own right married a Twisleton. A nineteenth century descendant of hers decided to bundle all the names together which gave us the surname of Twisleton-Wykeham-Fiennes. Fortunately, Dad paid a couple of quid to the post office to return to plain Fiennes.' This simplification cannot disguise the richness and complexity of the family story, read in the fabric and contents of the house. For Martin, the 'time machine' quality is central to what Broughton means. It combines national history, family history, domestic history and the history of objects and works of art. 'One of the lovely things is the layering,' says Martin. 'And,' he stresses, 'it's a beautiful place.'

There can be no arguing about that. The stone of the facade came from Hornton: Oxfordshire ironstone, whose ferrous content gives it the colour of marmalade; it turns orange in a good sunset. 'Obviously it's a much better colour than ordinary Cotswold stone,' observes Martin, with unashamed partiality. Over time, the face of the stone spalls and repairs will be needed. These were affected between 1982 and 1994, a twelve-year period during which scaffolding was never completely down from the house.

Really to understand the magic of this place you must go up to the roof. Below, in the castle garden, is a flower bed shaped like a fleur-de-lys; three swans glide over the surface of the moat; and beyond is as idyllic a view as it is possible to see in these islands. 'So I hope, almost more than anything, Broughton is an unspoilt rural paradise which says, "English countryside".'

It may not be to everyone's taste. Martin's wife Pauline and their three sons – Guy, Ned and Ivo – are, he says, 'more at home in the city'. A Singaporean, Pauline was a diplomat before her marriage, becoming First Secretary in the Singapore embassy in Washington, D.C. While she and the family 'love it, they live mostly in Oxford.' Which is not entirely to be wondered at. The kitchen at Broughton is an historic space that dates from the fourteenth century, complete with stone vault and corbels; the appliances, installed in the 1970s, are not the most modern. There are many enormous rooms in the castle and a lot of exposed stone. Repairs are constantly needed and never ending. 'One day at the end of an open day, the guide said there was a note for me. It read, "I have just graduated from the Courtauld doing a course in picture restoration and noticed that one or two of your paintings could benefit from attention." Katya Belaia started by doing a survey of all pictures, then prioritising the order to deal with them. She has done about sixty over five years.' She is still going. And once the pictures have been finished, there are the frames. Two from around 1680 were recently found to have been originally covered in silver leaf.

The history of this family has been a roller-coaster. Highs of political favour and riches have been followed by lows of extravagance and financial catastrophes. Over the internal porch by which the Oak Room is entered has been placed a Latin inscription. 'I scream with joy every time somebody not only translates it but also identifies where it originated; only two people have. It comes from the Aeneid. But whereas Virgil wrote "One day we will look back with pleasure on the memories of the past," the 8th Lord Saye and Sele changed it to: "There is no pleasure in memories of the past." A reference to his role as a Parliamentarian in the English Civil War. I love all that.'

By the Regency, the Puritanism of the 7th and 8th Barons had been forgotten. This was the era of William, 15th Lord Saye and Sele, born 1798, a Byronic figure who lived high. According to the Reminiscences of Captain [Rees] Gronow, 1862, he was an epicure, who once breakfasted on an omelette of golden pheasant's eggs, and hard drinker. When a new servant asked if he had any orders, he was told, as his lordship went into dinner: 'Place two bottles of sherry by my bed-side and call me the day after tomorrow.' These excesses did not take place at Broughton but at The Belvedere, a now demolished house on the south side of the Thames.

The 'naughty' 15th Lord never married. He was succeeded by his cousin, Frederick, the 16th Lord who husbanded the family fortune and refurbished the castle – hence the acquisition of armour from Samuel Pratt. Good Frederick, as Martin calls him, had taken Holy Orders and rose to become Archdeacon of Hereford Cathedral. Unfortunately, his heir, John, 18th Lord, had a weakness for the turf. Disaster. 'In a way, we applaud the hedonism. The family never had enough money during t he nineteenth century to turn Broughton into a Gothic Revival horror.'

Broughton had, in comparison to some country houses, a lenient Second World War. The Oak Room and great hall were piled from floor to ceiling with cases containing the insect collection from the Natural History Museum, moved out of London to protect them from

German bombs. After the War, Martin's great-grandfather, the 20th Baron, got a hundred per cent grant from the Historic Buildings Council to replace the roof, and Broughton's slow, strenuous revival began. One of the officials who visited to inspect the house left his papers behind. They contained the comment that the Twistleton-Wykeham-Fiennes family was 'notoriously impoverished.'

Fortunately for Broughton, Martin's father, Nathaniel, 21st Lord Saye and Sele, loved the place. A land agent by profession, he is now ninety-nine and still keenly interested in anything that concerns the Castle and the estate. He, his wife Mariette and their three, soon to be four children arrived in the late 1960s. These were, in every sense, uncomfortable years for the British stately home but they made a fist of it. The delight of growing up in a castle is captured in William Fiennes's *The Music Room*, a moving account of his eldest brother Richard's life and charisma, as well as the suffering caused by his severe epilepsy (Richard died in 2001). Lord and Lady Saye and Sele not only succeeded in passing the castle and estate on in good heart but have left a legacy in the form of furniture, commissioned from John Makepeace and Alan Peters, two of the best British designers of the late twentieth century.

Martin was seven when he came to live at Broughton. It was a thrilling place for him and his siblings to grow up. In time, he made the short journey to Oxford University, where he read Geography (his children, he says, tease him about it). He still spends most of the week at Oxford where he works for a tech venture capital fund. 'We invest in science coming out of the University of Oxford. Really exciting stuff is going on. I hope one of the sixty companies we've invested in will do so well it will pay for the new wallpaper needed in the long gallery, and much more. The work is amazing – just as living here is amazing.'

It was in 2014 that his parents moved out of the castle. For the previous fifteen years, they had been sharing the running of it with Martin. The transition happened without fuss. As to business, ... well there is little sign of rapaciously commercial activity, which is part of its charm. When a van delivering to an extravagant wedding that was held in the grounds knocked the corner of the early fourteenth-century gatehouse, Martin felt the damage to the old stone like a wound. While the aim is to make a profit from the house, the losses on it are covered by profits from the eighteen-hundred-acre estate. A question mark remains over the future of agriculture but useful extra revenue comes from filming. Little touched by the twentieth and twenty-first centuries, Broughton has been the location for the BBC series *Wolf Hall* and the feature films *Jane Eyre* (2011) and *Shakespeare in Love* (1998), featuring Martin's cousin Joseph Fiennes.

And the next generation? 'I hope that one day one of the boys will take over. I don't want them to think they have to do it. A lot will depend on what kind of jobs they get.' Their subjects are Arabic, international relations and psychology. 'It would be pointless staying on here if they were selling everything to keep it going. But that's for another day.'

For Martin, the next project is a coat of arms. There is a big one at parapet level, in the centre of the entrance front. Erected in 1550, it is now badly decayed. 'We have got prices for repairing it and for carving a new one. We've pretty much decided to put up a new one.' Originally it would have been brightly painted, and a new coat-of-arms could be again. 'Imagine – if you just had a splash of colour, in the middle of the stone façade. I'm rather excited by that.' Broughton has not lost the power to enthral this most intellectually curious of owners.

Martin Fiennes's brother William Fiennes called his book about growing up at Broughton *The Music Room*. It contains a moving description of their eldest brother Richard's life and charisma, as well as the suffering caused by his severe epilepsy.

This page & opposite, The great hall, with sofas upholstered in crimson plush made in the nearby village of Shutford at the turn of the twentieth century. Some of the medieval armour was bought for the castle in 1860 from the Bond Street dealer Samuel Pratt. The plaster was stripped from the walls to reveal the stonework around 1900.

The Oak Room, being restored to its usual condition after a party. Over the interior porch is a Latin inscription in which the 8th Lord Saye and Sele regrets the miseries of the English Civil War. The marine painting shows the Beach at Scheveningen, in Holland.

Opposite, Bedroom hung with Chinese wallpaper. The bed was commissioned by the present Lord and Lady Saye and Sele from Robin Furlong, one of a number of pieces of contemporary furniture in the house including work by John Makepeace and Alan Peters.

This page, The cartouche over the fireplace in the King's Chamber shows Dryads dancing around an oak tree, in a scene and style derived from the engravings and plasterwork at Fontainebleau.

This page & opposite, The early fourteenth-century Groined Passage, with corbel heads. The heads are like ones in the parish church, just beyond the gatehouse to Broughton, built by John de Broughton about 1300.

This page & opposite, Staircases in concrete, stone and wood. Opposite Pauline Fiennes stands at the bottom of a spiral stair boldly inserted in the 1970s: the unadorned concrete cantilevers complement the exposed stonework of the walls.

The many staircases are part of the romance of Broughton. The elm floorboards have an almost sensuous quality.

This page & opposite, Swans glide on the moat, while the best view of the fleurs-de-lys knot garden is obtained by passing birds.

Next spread, The church, the gatehouse, the castle, the Oxfordshire plain: 'I hope more than anything,' says Martin Fiennes, 'that it's an unspoilt rural paradise which says, "English countryside".'

THE HISTORY OF BROUGHTON CASTLE

In 2018, a metal detectorist discovered an ancient tile on a field near Broughton Castle. It was one thousand eight hundred years old and had belonged to a Roman hypocaust, or heating system. This was the first clue to the existence of a Roman villa on the site. Subsequent investigation revealed coins, pot sherds and the tusk of a very large wild boar – and showed that it was on a scale like that of Buckingham Palace. So as an inhabited site, Broughton Castle is even older than it appears from the surviving fabric of the house, significant parts of which date from the early fourteenth century.

The effigy of Sir John de Broughton, who built the castle, can be seen in the church beside the gatehouse. He died in 1315, having been granted free warren of Broughton in 1301. The original plan of Sir John's house is now difficult to disinter; but from his time, or soon after, date the gatehouse, the trefoil windows over the stables next to it (presumably for a lodging) and the surprisingly complicated Groined Passage. Sir John also built the church,

whose corbel heads – carvings of faces at the springing of the arches – are in the same style as those in the Groined Passage. Broughton's lofty, first-floor chapel was licenced in 1331. It still contains the original stone altar slab on stone brackets.

In 1377, Broughton was acquired by the all-powerful William of Wykeham, one of whose many works was New College, built at Oxford twenty-seven miles away. His great-nephew Sir Thomas Wykeham received a licence to crenelate (make battlements) in 1406; this involved the building of a defensive wall around the moated enclosure. Sir Thomas's daughter married the 2nd Lord Saye and Sele, a Yorkist who died at the Battle of Barnet in 1471. The three next heirs died young. Revenues accumulated and the 6th Lord – strictly, Sir Richard Fiennes, since he never attempted to establish his right to the title – married the heiress of a rich London merchant. He was a Protestant who did better under Queen Elizabeth than Queen Mary, and briefly represented the county in Parliament.

By 1554, the date on a chimney above the entrance front, Fiennes had begun to remodel the castle, giving the entrance front an appearance of regularity, with large mullion windows, five gables and a degree of symmetry (which did not extend to the back). He raised the roof to accommodate two new floors above the great hall. From this period are the spectacular early Renaissance chimney pieces in Queen Anne's bedchamber (so called because James I's queen, Anne of Denmark, slept in the room on visits in 1604 and 1608) and the King's Chamber.

Fiennes's son, also Sir Richard, re-established the title, becoming the 7th Lord. He created a Great Chamber, now the Great Parlour, with an elaborate ceiling of interlaced ribs, bosses and deep pendants. Beneath it is the Oak Room, panelled and with an interior porch. The 7th Lord's son, William, who became 1st Viscount, was a Puritan. Under the front of a company for the settlement of New England, Saye held secret meetings at Broughton, from which servants were banned – whose 'great noises and talking' caused astonishment. To Charles I he was Old Subtlety.

Although the 1st Viscount was on the winning side of the Civil War, Broughton was badly damaged after a siege following the nearby Battle of Edgehill. It was described by his granddaughter, the diarist Celia Fiennes as being 'much left to decay and ruine' in 1674.

The Viscountcy died out in the eighteenth century but the Barony was revived in favour of the female line. This project probably owed something to a showy and ambitious wife called Elizabeth Turner who had married a Twisleton; she may also have been behind the eighteenth-century campaign to upgrade the house, introducing the fashionable Strawberry Hill plasterwork some of which survives in the long gallery and the ceiling of the great hall.

From 1810 the house was let; presumably, it was not maintained, since by 1820 the coat-of-arms on the entrance front (now being recarved) had fallen down.

It was during the 14th Baron's time that the 1837 sale took place; ostensibly, the property was that of a tenant who had taken the house but it included a mass of family things, now difficult to separate out; among them were, purportedly, a Titian and a Velasquez. Everything went, the last lot being for a swan and her cygnets. (Some pieces appear to have been brought back by a local clergyman, acting for the family.) The crisis may not have been caused by the 14th Lord so much as his son, the future 15th Lord, a recklessly extravagant figure whose improvidence was nothing checked by his inheriting in 1844.

Three years later, however, Naughty William was dead and Good Frederick had succeeded him. A cousin of his predecessor, the 16th Lord Saye and Sele could not have been a more different character: a clergyman who became Archdeacon of Hereford Cathedral. He is a hero in the history of the house, commissioning George Gilbert Scott Junior to restore Broughton with such restraint that his hand is barely noticeable. But money for this work was short. Like other landed families, the Saye and Seles were hit by the long agricultural depression that began in the late 1870s; by the time of the 16th Lord's death in 1887, bankruptcy loomed. It was only averted by letting Broughton. The family did not return until 1912. Only when the 21st Lord moved into the house, with his wife and young family, in the 1970s was the backlog of repairs addressed. Once again it became a family home.

HOPETOUN
HOUSE

West Lothian

Lord Hopetoun on the octagonal staircase designed by Sir William Bruce, exuberantly carved with garlands by Alexander Eizat and fitted with trompe-l'oeil paintings by William McLaren of 1967.

Charlotte, daughter of the Duke of Argyll, has a favourite godfather. It is Andrew, Earl of Hopetoun, from one of Scotland's other great eighteenth-century country houses, Hopetoun House, who showed her how to enliven a lunch party by putting runner beans in one's nostrils; licking off any gravy is the trick to making them stay in place. This will seem an unlikely talent for a man who, in other respects, is a model of decorum and, having read physics at Oxford, spent part of his early career as quite literally a rocket scientist (he designed missiles for the electronics company GEC). That was in Cheshire, followed by London. Then, twenty-one years ago, he returned to Scotland, locating himself and his family in Philpstoun House – a seventeenth-century laird's house which even the usually restrained Canmore, part of Historic Environment Scotland, describes as 'utterly charming.'

The Philpstoun House years ended in 2006, when Andrew's father, the 4th Marquess of Linlithgow, then only sixty, decided to leave Hopetoun, offering Andrew and Skye the chance to live there while their four children – Olivia, Gina, Charles and Victor – were young. 'It was incredibly generous and we're very grateful,' says Andrew. Andrew himself had not grown up at the house, since it was at first still occupied by his grandfather and then his parents divorced, meaning that half his teenage holidays were spent with his mother and stepfather in England.

At thirty-six, he was relatively young for the responsibility of Hopetoun, and it was an unfamiliar challenge. But he was practical and skilled in project management. Now fifty, he not only knows Hopetoun intimately but has a good idea about a lot of Scotland's privately-owned country houses, castles and gardens through chairing Historic Houses Scotland. All the two hundred and fifty

properties that the organisation represents have something in common (the need to keep going), and yet all are different. Few places other than Hopetoun, I suspect, have a duck and her brood living in one of the inner courtyards. She appeared suddenly, with eleven chicks; Skye was quick to buy duck feed and mealy worms. Hopetoun is a big house. It is also big-hearted.

We could talk in the Red Drawing Room, one of the Great Apartments created by William Adam and his sons John and Robert; but we decide to stay in the kitchen, near a reviving kettle. Kitchens are the heart of all modern houses, but this kitchen, characteristically for Hopetoun, is not quite as others. It is fairly large, naturally – Hopetoun is itself, by normal standards, vast (although it is slightly smaller than might appear, since the impression of size is exaggerated by the quadrant wings embracing the forecourt, which are really only one room deep). But Skye is firm in her dislike of expensive cabinetwork and state of the art gadgets. 'Did I want a big modern kitchen?' she asks rhetorically. 'Not really. I didn't want anyone to come in and think that we had done something.' She did enlarge the kitchen that Andrew's American step-grandmother had installed in the 1970s by fifty percent, installing a large table and a stone sink from a cottage on the estate, but the result is intentionally unglossy. 'After we'd finished, friends would come in and ask, "When are you starting?" I took it as a badge of distinction. A big kitchen suite means you don't use other rooms. People kept saying, "Why don't you put your kitchen on the floor above?" But I didn't want to ruin any of the smart rooms on the piano nobile.' That captures something of the family attitude to the house. 'It's like being a curator,' says Skye, 'trying not to balls it up.' Like other houses in this book, Hopetoun is owned by a preservation trust, of which Andrew is deputy chairman and resident trustee.

It is a principle at Hopetoun that every room is used on a regular basis. For Andrew, this is about more than simply enjoying the house where they live. 'People are here all the time, so you hope – touch wood – that some incipient disaster would be noticed. If there's a storm in the middle of the night, one gets up to check.' So as many rooms as possible should have a use and purpose. Far more of the house is used, says Skye, than in her father-in-law's time. 'We are a family of six before we even begin. We spread more.' Occupying the State rooms has become easier since the ropes were taken down 'We typically have thirty or so people staying for Christmas and the New Year and we use all of the house,' says Andrew. Skye admits to getting carried away with the Christmas trees. Last year Hopetoun had six.

A great innovation was a corridor of children's rooms. 'We wanted to make them feel as comfortable as possible.' Beyond that, the ruling principle as regards the historic fabric has been 'not to do very much.' Not that they have been idle: far from it. The last dozen or so years have been far busier than either of them had expected. For Andrew, house and estate must be juggled with other responsibilities, such as trusteeships, that are often unpaid. November is a particularly busy month due to the number of board meetings.

After the Second World War, Hopetoun was in poor shape. While the house escaped bombing, it suffered collateral damage: hot shrapnel from anti-aircraft fire fell on the lead of the roofs, which was already perishing. The lead was replaced but only with felt – a poor substitute which itself had to be renewed after a few decades. 'The twentieth century,' says Andrew, 'was a difficult period.' But the last twenty years has seen a transformation, both in Hopetoun's viability and attitudes in general. 'People used to ask, "What on earth is the point of these places?" Now they say what fantastic places these are. I think it is a very positive time.

The older generation used to say – "What! You live in the big house?" As though we were either mad or eccentric. People of our age don't seem at all surprised that we should be living here.'

Each year, sixty thousand visitors enjoy Hopetoun in one form or another, which is little in comparison to Inveraray, let alone Edinburgh Castle (two million visitors). Of those, thirty thousand or so pay to go around the house as day visitors. 'We try to be more than a visitor attraction because of where we are, near Edinburgh, and we have a ball room that seats three hundred people. That means we can play host to corporate events and weddings, which generate much more income while having far less impact on the house.' Fireworks nights can attract an audience of five thousand. On top of which are numerous school visits, on which primary school classes come and dress up as Victorian servants. With income from paying visitors and private events, the house pays for itself. Major campaigns of repair may need help from other sources. 'The Clothworkers' Foundation has been very helpful. They paid for a new loom for the volunteers who come and work on the tapestries. We have created a conservation studio at the north end of the house.' The Outlander stories, historic time-traveller books by Diana Gabaldon that have become several successful television series, have been an unexpected boon. 'Hopetoun has been one of the locations. The shell of a tower house near where my father lives that never had a visitor can now attract twenty thousand a year. That's amazing, but can create its own headaches, not least for the two families who live nearby.' Andrew can see social media and the internet have changed tourism. 'It has become more about the highlights – people come with the ten best things to see and work through them, in a way they would not have done twenty years ago. It leaves plenty of room to expand things nearby which may be every inch as interesting as a visitor attraction.'

Property remains a cornerstone of the estate. 'I have tried to make the property portfolio of sufficient size to become a manageable asset. It must be big enough to attract the right people to run it and to absorb maintenance costs. That's true of a lot of rural businesses; they need scale.'

Sentiment towards country houses in Scotland can be colder than that south of the Border. Romantic nationalists can be instinctively anti-laird – an attitude that sometimes expresses itself in the Scottish Parliament. 'Landownership can be an occasionally charged and emotive issue in Scotland,' says Andrew. 'But the family doesn't own the house – it's an independent charity.' Furthermore, heritage tourism 'is incredibly important to the Scottish economy. Figures from Visit Scotland show that two-thirds of visitors say that they have come to visit old houses or castles, or because of the landscape. This is well understood by our legislators.'

The out-of-doors is where Andrew recharges his mental batteries. 'I was down in London last week. I came home via a friend of mine in County Durham. We went out to walk the hill in the evening and got up for the blackcock lek. We walked out onto the hill and found a couple of curlew nests. I don't do that nearly as much as I'd like. It's very wonderful when it does happen. To get up at 4.30am and sit in a hide to watch this spectacle of Nature – and let the mind wander. It's very valuable.'

Skye's domain is the old kitchen garden. Walled, it covers twelve acres and had been used as a garden centre before Skye took it on. 'It had been fairly ruthlessly tidy,' says Skye. 'It is now rather less tidy but rather more rewarding.' Pesticides are banished. The only weed killer is a bit of glyphosate applied to the gravel paths (there are limits). 'The difference is huge. At the beginning, there were no worms in the soil. Now I don't ever dig without seeing worms.

Everything is improving. There had been no birdsong – no insect life at all. I tolerate what people used to call weeds. Our view of what's appropriate has changed.'

Much of the gardening is done by Skye herself, with the assistance of Caryn Farquhar who comes three days a week – and a thirty-year old pony (Andrew's mother breeds Shetlands) who eats the grass on a free-range basis. The task can be daunting but, Skye says, 'I do what I can. There would very rarely be a day when I don't manage at least an hour. There are times when I can do a whole day. There's an awful lot of it. So I don't let myself mind about things. It is what it is. Most of the box hedging was grown from tiny, tiny, tiny sprigs ten years ago. Nothing has gone in big. I see what it's going to be. It doesn't bother me that yews aren't big and round – they will be. Eventually everything will grow into each other so you won't be able to see paths.' Compost is practically a religion. 'The result is that when you walk in here in late summer, it is alive with insects. Heaving with them – the noise!'

Thirteen years – the time that Andrew and Skye have been at Hopetoun – may be, in some people's book, a long time; but their life's project of keeping Hopetoun humming, financially and culturally, horticulturally and hospitably, seems barely to have begun. It is only in rare moments of calm that they realise how much they have achieved. To quote Skye, 'Every so often we think, we've got so far to go. Then we look back and think we've come a long way.'

Skye Hopetoun's great joy is the walled garden, which covers twelve acres. It was previously let to a garden centre. 'It had been fairly ruthlessly tidy,' she says. 'It is now rather less tidy but rather more rewarding.' Pesticides are banned and the noise of insects can be 'deafening'.

Skye, Andrew and their elder son, Charles, in the kitchen which represents the family's big change at Hopetoun. Skye did not want anyone to think it was new.

Opposite, The junior corridor. A priority for Andrew and Skye on moving into Hopetoun in 2006 was to ensure their children, Olivia, Gina, Charles and Victor, had good bedrooms.

This page, Old-fashioned cupboards evoke country-house hospitality and routine at their most appealing.

The State Dining Room, created from a bedroom and anteroom in 1821; King George IV lunched in it the next year on turtle soup and three glasses of wine.

The pier glass and
pier table were made
for the Great or Red
Drawing Room in 1766
supervised by James
Cullen of London.
The marble for the pier
tables was ordered by
Robert Adam while he
was in Italy in 1755.

Tapestry and oak panelling
in a spare bedroom.

Scenes from the attics; Hopetoun is a
palimpsest of many ages.

Previous spread, Eleven miles from Edinburgh, beside the Firth of Forth, Hopetoun began life as a compact house built by the architect Sir William Bruce in 1698-1702 for the 1st Earl of Hopetoun. Lord Hopetoun was then a minor and the project was driven by his mother, Lady Margaret Hope. To this Lord Hopetoun added quadrant wings and pavilions between 1721-46, to the design of William Adam.

Opposite: Skye gathers apples in the walled garden. For Skye and Andrew the outdoors acts as a tonic during busy lives.

This page: Skye and Charles walking in the Avenue.

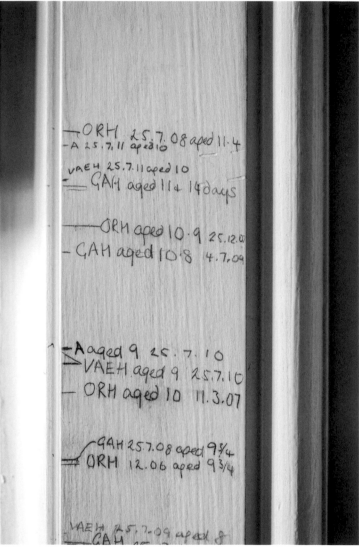

Left, Who needs social media to stay in touch with family events when there's a pin board?

Right, New heights reached by the children are marked on the wall.

Opposite, Closely hung with old family photographs, festooned with antlers and all-weather clothing and with a dog bed under the sink, the boot room is a hymn to the outdoors.

THE HISTORY OF
HOPETOUN HOUSE

Hopetoun House was built to stun. The entrance front looks towards the Firth of Forth (and today's elegant Queensferry Crossing bridge) and enfolds the visitor in the arms of two quadrant wings, ending in pavilions; like the courtship display of a peacock, the object is less to welcome than to impress. In this it succeeds. Hopetoun is regarded as Scotland's most handsome country house in the Classical style, following the demolition of Hamilton Palace in the 1920s.

The man who built it, Charles Hope, 1st Earl of Hopetoun, came from a family of lawyers. He was only a baby when his father died in 1682. When the lengthy contract to erect the mansion was put before Edinburgh's finest craftsmen in the last days of 1698, it was Hope's 'curators' or trustees who signed it; the driving force was his mother, Lady Margaret, a daughter of the 4th Earl of Haddington. Lady Margaret renounced control of her son's affairs in 1700, leaving him – in the words of his architect, Sir William Bruce – in possession of 'a plentiful free fortun ... no father, no brother, no sisters burdensome upon ye Estate'.

When the client had his portrait painted, he was shown either in armour or robes of State; he was a politician who supported the Union during the years of Jacobite rebellion and in 1721 received a large payment from the secret service fund. When Bruce was painted in 1664, by contrast, he chose to appear in a multicoloured dressing gown, regarding the spectator with an imperious stare, mitigated by the faint smile that curls his sensualist's rosebud lips. The pencil line of moustache on his upper lip, so thin as to be barely visible, indicates a man who took a dandyish care of his appearance. This debonair individual played a key role in the Restoration of Charles II. As chaos descended after Cromwell's death in 1658, he appears to have persuaded General Monck to support the return of the Stuarts, and then to have acted as intermediary with the exiled court. After the Restoration, Bruce's star soared. He became a baronet, a Privy Councillor of Scotland, a collector of fines and taxes, and the Surveyor of the King's Works in Scotland. In 1681-93, he built himself a suave and imaginative country house – Kinross House, twenty-five miles North of Edinburgh – which set a new bar for sophistication in Scotland, introducing a restrained but sumptuous classical style, strongly influenced by France.

By the late 1690s, however, Bruce's star was in decline. Owing everything to the Stuarts, he became a persona non grata at court after the abdication of James II. Kinross was never fully completed and he was under constant suspicion of being a Jacobite. As Bruce wrote prophetically of Hopetoun, 'its like to be ye last of any considerable work of mine'.

In *Vitruvius Britannicus*, 1717, Colen Campbell describes Hopetoun as possessing 'a Portico, Hall and 4 very handsome Apartments…over the Hall is a noble Salon and the same Number of Apartments as below, and all well finished and sumptuously furnished'. The plan of the main block was a Greek cross, with an octagonal staircase hall in the centre; according to an account by John Macky, written in 1723, it was 'finely adorned with the History of the Heathen Gods, done at Antwerp and put into Pannels from top to bottom': a scheme that has now disappeared. Externally this was marked by a tall cupola, like the dome at Castle Howard. On either side of the house, Lord Hopetoun and his wife, Lady Henrietta, only daughter of the first Marquess of Annandale, had mirroring apartments – bedchamber, dressing room and closet – in the manner expected of royalty and Baroque grandees. They formed a sequence of rooms that got ever richer, culminating in the closets which had corner fireplaces.

Outside, Bruce's quadrant wings were designed to be convex, rather than concave. It is doubtful that they were built, since the present, conventionally Palladian (concave) quadrants date from the 1720s, when the now ennobled Earl had his house made even grander by William Adam. (Bruce had died, in relative obscurity, in 1710.) Adam also increased the size of the main block by a bay to either side, altered the skyline by adding a parapet which hides the cupola, and built two pavilions, one to contain stables and the other, a library and billiard room. The Earl may not have been best pleased with the relationship that he had with his busy architect, to judge from a letter written by Lord Annandale to Sir John Clerk: 'as for Adams, he has so many Real and so many Imaginary projects, that he minds nobody, nor no thing to purpose.' On the Earl's death in 1742, the house had yet to be finished, since the masons were only discharged in 1746, and even then the staircase that forms the centrepiece of the entrance façade had yet to be built. When William Adam died in 1748, work was continued by his sons, John, Robert and James. The personable and socially ambitious Robert would travel in Italy with the 2nd Earl's brother Charles Hope.

Although Hopetoun had been building for over forty years, the Adam brothers were given, internally, a blank canvas. The Earl's Great or North Apartment was an unfurnished shell. Rich and somewhat conservative in taste (Robert Adam had yet to develop the brilliant decorative repertoire he derived from his studies in Italy), the interiors are today unusually complete. Most of the Adam furniture remains in the house, along with the silk damask wall-hangings of the Red Drawing Room, smuggled into the country to avoid taxes. The majority was supplied by Edinburgh craftsmen, or even made on the Hopetoun estate. The Yellow Drawing Room was originally the Great Dining Room. The present dining room was created from the Great Apartment's bedchamber and dressing room for the visit of George IV in 1822.

In the 1990s much of this precious ensemble of contents at Hopetoun was acquired by the Hopetoun Foundation with the help of the National Heritage Memorial Fund.

FIRLE
PLACE

East Sussex

The Hon. Henry Gage with Phoebe in the staircase hall at Firle Park in Sussex, inserted around 1720.
Henry has recently moved into the house.

Pass the gates at Firle Place and you enter an enchanted kingdom. First come what old-fashioned authors called the 'sylvan charms' of the park, flat but embellished with a great variety of different trees. When the house appears, it stands against a shoulder of the South Downs, in a creamy coloured stone that has been dusted with brown lichen. It is Georgian without being symmetrical, somewhat French but in the most English of settings. The delicacy and refinement continue inside, where the walls are hung with outstanding family portraits between cabinets displaying Sèvres porcelain. This is a connoisseur's house; inside it, aesthetic harmony rules. In a museum, the result might be stiff, but here enjoyment of the many works of art, some of which are outstanding, is enhanced by the relaxed attitude of a family for whom beautiful objects have been part of the background to life for generations.

But what is this? I visit on a day when the pictures are being taken down from the walls. Strong men are carrying furniture into a state room that has been temporarily designated for storage. The lovely interior is being systematically dismantled. The 8th Viscount Gage, aged eighty-five, and his son Henry, some forty years younger, look on philosophically, as they discuss the colours that the walls will eventually be repainted once the film production company has gone. Because Firle is being repurposed as a location for a remake of Jane Austen's *Emma*. This seems eminently appropriate. Although the scenographers require the place to be stripped, so that, for their eleven-week stay, a new décor can be created, Firle always seems to be an embodiment of the unshowy refinement and gentlemanly consideration for others of which Austen approved. This may be an illusion. Like other houses, Firle has passed through many phases of existence since the Regency. But since 1993, when Lord Gage, known as Nicky, inherited

from his brother George, 7th Viscount, the house has been in the hands of what Henry describes as 'a figure from before the Industrial Revolution – a proper gentleman from the eighteenth century.'

Born in 1934, some of Nicky's earliest memories are associated with Firle, where his first years were spent. But for two years during the Second World War, he was evacuated to Wales ('I adored that'). Firle, only a few miles from the south coast, was in danger of being bombed; besides, it was needed by the army for D-Day preparations – so secret that, when the threat of bombing had receded and the Gages moved back to a farmhouse on the estate, they were not allowed to walk in the park. Those times of restricted movement would be forever seared on Nicky's memory. 'I still feel it's a great treat to go to Newhaven and even more to take a ferry to France.' We talk in the kitchen, its dresser plastered with rosettes won at Pony Club events by Nicky's ten-year-old son by his second marriage, John. ('I am the oldest father in the world.') Across the corridor is a playroom, full of rocking horses, drum kits and painting materials. Creativity is nurtured at Firle. In the service courtyard, a double-height space, stripped to the brick and lit from both sides, is a studio. It is where Nicky paints. How could he not? A mile away from the house when he was growing up were the Bloomsbury Group, whose country headquarters was the old farmhouse of Charleston. Nicky used to see Vanessa Bell and her husband Clive when he walked over. 1952 was a great year in the history of Firle. It was then that the Cowper collection arrived: works of art of the highest quality, many of them bought by the 3rd Earl of Cowper who had spent thirty years of the eighteenth century living in Florence. They included (left to the 3rd Earl by his grandfather, the Earl of Grantham) van Dyke's magnificent group portait of *John, Count of Nassau-Siegen with his Family* that hangs in the great hall.

Nicky returned to the house after his father's death in 1983. 'My brother George – he was a well-known eccentric: I was very fond of him but he wasn't quite like others – didn't want to live here at first. As time passed, he changed his mind. He felt he should do so. And so he did. It made him overcome his fear of ghosts, because Firle is rather haunted.' Nicky retreated into a smaller area of the house and was about to move out when George died in 1993. By now he had two children from his first wife, Henry and Ben, born in 1975 and 1977, although the marriage had broken up; the boys, having grown up at Firle, could continue to stay there.

Like other landowners, Nicky suffered during the Lloyds crisis of the 1990s; it was therefore decided that Firle needed a maintenance fund. Heritage Maintenance Funds provide a means of protecting capital, set aside for the repair of listed buildings, from tax. Fortunately for the Firle trustees, the Getty Museum in California had entered the art market, using its spectacular endowment to buy Old Masters and other works of art. It acquired Fra Bartolommeo's *The Rest on the Flight into Egypt with St. John the Baptist*, painted in 1509, for £14 million. Firle could now position itself for the future, preserving both house and collection.

While the maintenance fund can make a substantial contribution towards Firle's annual repair bill, it cannot cover the big-ticket items. 'We've just spent one and a half million on the roof,' comments Nicky, 'and you wouldn't even notice it.' These burdens are now shared with Henry, Lord Gage's eldest son, who now lives in the house: Nicky and his wife Alexandra have withdrawn to a wing, while making their main home in a restored farmhouse (the one in which Nicky spent some of the Second World War). 'It's Henry's chance now. We are partially going away to let him blossom. I'm sure he will.'

Sharing a house is not a domestic formula that would work for all families but, at Firle, father and son share the same values. 'You have to remember that I'm not married and don't yet have children,' says Henry. There will be an element of unfamiliarity to the new order, but then transition was not an issue much faced by previous generations, when people died younger. In those days, inheritance generally came whilst eldest sons were still young, or relatively so. 'The Gages have always tended to marry older; they have children in their forties rather than twenties.'

While Nicky is a farmer, Henry has other interests. At Bristol University, he took a degree in Latin American Studies and Spanish. Then came a period of work experience at Grimsthorpe, then a very traditional estate. 'When I came back from there, I went into business with a chum of mine and for ten years we built up a company that cultivated hemp seed and produced food for Sainsbury's. Hemp oil, hemp pasta, hemp ice cream.' Eventually it was sold and Henry returned to Firle: 'I didn't have the imagination to do anything else. Since then I've been here getting involved with the bits of the estate that I like.' And what he loves is building up the events. Channel 4's *Bake Off: The Professionals* has been filmed at Firle every year since the second series. The riding school has been converted into a display kitchen, while the editing suite is in the stables.

There is already a microbrewery in the village, and Henry would like to develop other businesses in food and wine – if he could find the investment. 'There are lots of really interesting things we could do. It's the perfect place to establish a vineyard. With that would come a visitor element, as happens at other English vineyards.' Recently he was approached by a company that wants to take five acres of forest and build tree houses.

Other projects include holiday lets. Henry also runs a clay shoot, and a barn has been converted for *Hunter Gather Cook*, which offers cooking courses. 'With the right kind of events, the whole place starts singing.'

With its seven thousand acres, the Firle estate is one of the biggest in the south-east of England. While owning most of the village as well as other residential property, it does not maximise rents. 'My father's wish – and I fully support him – is for the housing to be accessible.' Tenants are more likely to be yoga teachers or artists than City slickers: 'we certainly don't want commuters,' says Nicky. Families with children get a discount, which supports the village school. This creates, says Henry, 'a great atmosphere in the village – even if it's not so great for the balance sheet.' While other pretty villages in East Sussex, occupied by well-to-do retirees, exhibit little sense of community, Firle is a whirl of activity.

The pressure for new homes near London must surely mean that the Firle estate can provide building sites? Wrong. The creation of the South Downs National Park in 2011 scotched that possibility. Even affordable housing is hard to get through the planning system. Outside the National Park can be even more difficult than within it.

'Fifteen years ago we were approached by Wealden District Council who wanted six hundred houses to be constructed; we were not very keen – it might have spoiled the character of the area. This scheme was pared down to twenty-five to thirty dwellings. But we have not been able to get planning permission even for them.'

But the National Park helps preserve the beauty of the South Downs, and that is all part of the Firle offering. 'It's a beautiful place,' says Henry, 'but not Blenheim Palace. We have six thousand visitors and it's difficult to imagine there being many more. The house offers nothing for kids. Instead, people come here to go for a walk on the Downs, or to get married, or go to Glyndebourne. Perhaps they have a meal in the pub or come back to hold a corporate event.'

Firle is a delicate and special organism; its character cannot be easily defined. 'It's not a brand like a kind of toothpaste.' Standards are important: the public should be able to trust Firle to do everything to the highest level. It must also set an example in its use of natural resources. 'Only a century ago, Firle would have been totally self-sufficient in food, power and water. We can reinstate this model. We're at quite an advanced state in planning a district heating system for the village. The house has a wood burner, using wood chip from our woods. We've halved the heating bill. We think that sixty per cent of the village could be heated from ground source, and we are looking at another wood burner to serve the rest. We have tenants who use our water supply, for which we charge a little bit less than a water company.'

Like other estate owners, the Gages take a long view. 'We've been here for five hundred years,' says Nicky, 'and hope to be here for the next five hundred.' How does Henry feel as he takes over the reins? 'I have a big feeling that I don't want to screw it up. I've been given this opportunity and I choose to do it because it's fun and creative. But you don't want to be the one who drops the ball.'

Nicky, 8th Viscount Gage and his wife Alexandra in the
Palladian drawing room, hung with family portraits.
Unusually, the circular one over the chimneypiece
is set into a frame of looking glass.

Opposite, Firle from the park. Behind it rises Firle Beacon, a high point of the South Downs: beyond it is the sea. The estate of seven thousand acres is one of the largest in the South-East.

This page, The cream-coloured, faintly-yellow limestone gives Firle a French look.

Opposite, The hall displays van Dyke's monumental portrait *John, Count of Nassau-Siegen with his Family* of 1634. This came to Firle after the Second World War as part of the Cowper collection, formed in the eighteenth century by the 3rd Earl of Cowper who rarely returned to England after his Grand Tour having fallen in love with a Marchesa in Florence. The van Dyke is the greatest of glories in a house that contains many and varied beautiful things – Georgian paintings, furniture by Chippendale and Gillows, sixteenth-century majolica tiles from Antwerp, Beauvais tapestries … the list goes on.

Left, The Pink Bedroom. Guests can safely stay here because, unlike the Blue Bedroom, it is not haunted.

Right, The Library houses an important collection of books and manuscripts including Gerardus Mercator's *Atlas* dated 1591-3; a first edition of the Elizabethan doctor, William Gilbert's *De Magnete* (On Magnetism), circa 1600; and 'The Curse of Minerva' by Lord Byron, dedicated in his hand to Lady Caroline Lamb in 1812.

The Hon. John Gage, a pensive equestrian. The kitchen dresser at Firle is covered in the rosettes won at Pony Club events.

Father and son set off for a hack. The stables and riding school are Regency; the latter now contains display kitchens for the television series, *Bake Off: The Professionals*.

Horses are a passion at Firle.
The old parkland turf makes
ideal going for the horse trials
that are often held here.

Opposite & this page, The youngest son John's presence in the kitchen (notice rosettes), playroom and corridors at Firle is unmistakable. Country houses have a lot of space for creativity.

Nicky in his studio. As boys, he and his brother George would visit the Bloomsbury Group at Charleston, which is on the Firle estate a few miles from the big house. 'Duncan Grant was never known to say anything rude about somebody's painting so we always asked his advice.'

OLD HOMES, NEW LIFE

Where sheep may safely graze. Under the stewardship of the Gages, Firle remains a rare piece of Arcadia in an increasingly busy part of England, now within the curtilage of the South Downs National Park.

THE HISTORY OF
FIRLE PLACE

Firle Place was originally a Tudor house; it was, as it were, gift-wrapped in the mid-eighteenth century and, at various points, filled with exquisite bonbons in the form of portraits and porcelain. The pale limestone – a cream colour, dusted with brown lichen – gives it a French look, but formality struggles against the underlying irregularity of the old building which keeps breaking out.

In the sixteenth century, Sir John Gage had a house here, containing a hall, chapel, great parlour, little parlour, nursery and two wardrobes, as well as a kitchen, buttery, dairy and brewhouse. As a young man, he served in Henry VII's household as Esquire of the Body, and he continued to be a courtier under Henry VIII. But he was principally distinguished as 'one of the wisest and most experienced in war of the whole kingdom.' He resigned from the King's Council over Henry's divorce from Catherine of Aragon; later, however, he was made Comptroller of the Household and Governor of the Tower of London, witnessing the execution of Lady Jane Grey.

He was at Firle when he died in 1556.

The house had two courts, separated by the hall. Although only one gable from Sir John's time can still be seen, the courts remain, albeit altered and beneath later cladding. A Tudor fireplace and part of a wallpainting exist in the dining room, and the hammer beam roof of the hall also survives, although it can only be seen by visiting the attics: from below, it is concealed by a deeply coved plaster ceiling. Sir John's will mentions an exceptional number of feather beds – 40 – as well as his own campaign furniture: 'Myn owne taynte for the feld with the Tymber to the same.' This came with a field kitchen and buttery, a tent for captains, a stable, and a little tent for a surgeon. When Sir John's grandson, also John, erected the Gage chapel at Firle church in the 1590s, he commissioned the sculptor Garret Johnson (1541-1611) of Southwark to carve effigies of Sir John and his wife Philippa; he is shown wearing his Garter sash.

The Gage family remained Catholics; this prevented them from playing a role in national affairs and there is no evidence that they did very much to alter Sir John's house. In 1695, Sir William Gage, 7th Baronet, became a Protestant, perhaps to sit in Parliament as member for Seaford; he was awarded the Order of the Bath. History remembers him for introducing the greengage from France – hence the name. Sir William died unmarried in 1744, and Firle passed to his cousin Thomas, who had been created 1st Viscount Gage in 1720. Since this is an Irish peerage, Lord Gage could continue to sit in Parliament as an MP, using his position to expose the fraudulent sale of the Derwentwater Estates (the property of the 3rd Earl of Derwentwater, confiscated when he was beheaded for his role in the 1715 Jacobite rebellion). For this he was awarded £2,000. It is now difficult to know whether the remodelling of Firle was undertaken by Sir William Gage or the 1st Viscount; there is no documentary evidence. If the work of the 1st Viscount, it would have been old-fashioned – but then the failure to overcome the episodic nature of the Tudor house suggests that the architect responsible (we do not know who this was) was probably not a sophisticated figure from London and may have been behind the times.

The lack of symmetry in no way detracts from Firle's charm. Externally, the windows are surrounded by stone bands rather than carved architraves, giving them the effect of having been punched into the walls – a treatment that looks radical now but may have been occasioned by lack of money. Firle is entered from the narrow east front. A rusticated gateway with a Palladian window above gives into one of the Tudor courts, reduced in size by the addition of corridors. On the further side of the court, the front door is off centre and gives into the great hall. The staircase hall is to the left, the stair itself rising, at a shallow angle, around three sides of it – a form that was popular in the Stuart period.

The hall contains the greatest of the many glories of Firle: van Dyke's monumental portrait of *John, Count of Nassau-Siegen with his Family*, painted during a visit to Brussels in 1634. This came to Firle after the Second World War as part of the Cowper collection. The core of the collection had been formed by the 3rd Earl of Cowper who, as Lord Fordwich, arrived in Florence in 1759, while making his Grand Tour, and decided to stay there; he had fallen in love both with the city and the Marchesa Corsi. Not even a seat in the House of Commons, engineered by his father, could persuade him to return. We see the 3rd Earl, hat raised, in a portrait by Johann Zoffany, who advised him on art purchases in Florence; a view of Florence appears in the background.

The 7th Earl Cowper inherited some of Thomas Chippendale's finest pieces, the Panshanger Cabinets, as well as a superb collection of porcelain, particularly Sèvres, some of it commissioned directly from the factory by the 1st Viscount Melbourne. The Cowper Collection arrived from Panshanger in Hertfordshire on the death of the present Lord Gage's grandmother, the hostess Ettie, Lady Desborough, who had been one of the aristocratic intellectuals, aesthetes and advanced thinkers known as The Souls. If the Second World War had caused Firle to be transformed in an unhappy though temporary way, this magnificent inheritance changed its appearance in an altogether more welcome and more permanent manner. Panshanger was sold to a demolition contractor, to become one of the lost country houses of the dark post-War decades.

GRIMSTHORPE CASTLE

Lincolnshire

Sebastian and Emma Miller, on right, with children Merlin and Hermione,
in the Vanbrugh Hall at Grimsthorpe Castle.

Sebastian and Emma Miller have just moved into a flat in Grimsthorpe Castle. Once, Grimsthorpe would have been a true castle, but, largely under the hand of Sir John Vanbrugh in 1715, it became a splendid country house – forbidding (as the first syllable of the name suggests) but fantastic, even playful. Since 1983, it has been home to Jane, the 28th Lady Willoughby de Eresby, who has run both the castle and the fifteen thousand acre Lincolnshire estate as a model of their kind: everything under the eye of the severed Saracen's head that is the Willoughby de Eresby crest being of the best. And this is true not only of Grimsthorpe but Drummond Castle in Perthshire, Lady Willoughby's Scottish property, famous for its immaculate formal gardens. But change is afoot. What could once operate as private homes, along strictly traditional lines, now must rely on their own resources to generate the income to keep them going. Sebastian, as the resident trustee of the Grimsthorpe and Drummond Castle Trust and Lady Willoughby's first cousin once removed, is charged with the delicate task of opening Grimsthorpe a little more to the world, without compromising its prestige and mystique. At present, Grimsthorpe has only two thousand visitors a year inside the house.

Sebastian comes to Grimsthorpe from the Blues and Royals, which he joined on leaving school. His last role was at Warminster, training young officers and soldiers in the tactics of reconnaissance and surveillance. 'Before that I had been seconded to the French army. I was sent on a language course for eight months, in the expectation of being sent to help defeat jihadism and stop the stream of refugees from Africa. I lived in Tours. Then Mali blew up and the French decided to deploy at short notice.' Sebastian went with them to Mali as liaison officer. 'I loved Mali. I found the idea of a wooden shack under a few mango trees very appealing.'

Grimsthorpe is 'quite a contrast.' Not that the organisation of an estate is so different from his army experience. 'You have the same HR issues, the same dramas. It's just that you're overcoming them with grown-ups, not young men.' The greatest difference is that Grimsthorpe is now home. 'Throughout our married life we have, until now, been nomadic. We moved twenty times. In the army, you are used to being completely stripped down to the bare essentials of living – three sets of underpants, two pairs of socks, two shirts, a pair of trousers and a suitcase.' They moved every two years. To Emma, it was 'quite odd suddenly coming here and being part of a very close-knit community.' A generation ago, Grimsthorpe had been no less a challenge to Lady Willoughby. As a girl, she had not expected the responsibility: it fell to her after the death of her brother Timothy in 1963, when his motorboat sank amid storms in the Mediterranean. 'She was a woman on her own, with no husband or immediate family to bounce ideas off,' says Emma. 'She has kept it going in the most amazing way, which has been extraordinary for a woman surrounded by men. She has an incredible memory and eye for detail. She will pick up on anything that's out of place, even in a place that she has not visited for decades.' Having been a train bearer and maid of honour to Queen Elizabeth II during her coronation in 1953, Lady Willoughby de Eresby was also a significant presence in the artistic world of the 1960s. A friend and patron of Francis Bacon, Frank Auerbach and Michael Andrews, she was particularly close to Lucian Freud. In *Breakfast with Lucian*, Geordie Greig describes her as his 'most loyal patron, supporter, friend, lover, muse and soulmate,' who often rescued him from the consequences of his passion for gambling.

Sebastian believes that Grimsthorpe's offering to visitors must be improved in line with the potential. 'We want to up our game.' Until now, Grimsthorpe has been 'a quiet estate' with a restaurant whose primary function is to fulfil the Charity Commission's objectives that food should be offered as part of the terms of the Trust. 'We will need a restaurant that is open in the evenings and able to satisfy the tastes of the people who come to see the amazing collection in the gallery. The days of sleepy Grimsthorpe just serving a curled sandwich and a cup of tea are over. We might also have a good, up-to-the-minute adventure park, at a distance from the house. We are only ten minutes from the A1 and have excellent rail connections to London from Peterborough and Grantham.' As footfall increases, other projects will become possible: Sebastian has his eye on a derelict pub that could perhaps be turned into a small hotel. These projects are part of a vision for the entire Grimsthorpe estate. 'We've got to make it work as a whole, and we can't move forward without change.' Shooting is 'not vitally important for income but it's important in other ways. It employs someone to be a keeper. That means providing supplementary feeding and vermin control – as a result of which wildlife does better. We have some amazing woods; they're principally oak woods – some of the oldest in the country. There are several Sites of Special Scientific Interest, with extremely rare plants and butterflies; some of them can be found only here and nowhere else.' These are things that would excite the public if they knew about them. 'Because of the interest in Nature, we employ a ranger now and perhaps could expand the service. Or get volunteers involved.'

One of the SSSIs is the park around Grimsthorpe itself, planted by Capability Brown in two campaigns – one for the 2nd Duke of Ancaster in 1741-2, the other for the latter's son the 3rd Duke thirty years later. The park is farmed by a tenant, who grows 'wheat, barley and rape, with some pulses thrown in.

The rest is grass, and almost organic. It must be grazed by a native British animal – in this case, Longhorns crossed with Aberdeen Angus. Longhorns are best at getting into heavy grass and keeping it down. And they're really good to eat.' Recently, trees have been cut down around the lake to restore the landscape to the condition that Brown intended. The water in the lake has been improved, giving more oxygen to fish. 'The views from the castle to the lake and vice-versa are now fabulous.' Until now, the park has not been considered as a revenue generator but that could change. 'There could be more interesting things to go and see in the park, such as modern sculptures or small arboretums; I would like to create little gardens by the lake. This year we are doing five or six major events which would have been unheard of five years ago. The Baston Car Show attracted an audience of a thousand people. There soon will be a forest festival in one of the woods on the estate; some people would call it a rave – a highly organised rave, that is. Events like that will test our security systems – and test our patience. But we need to test them. In years to come we can do something crazier, bigger, more exciting.'

Grimsthorpe also has a portfolio of rental property. Many tenants come from families who have lived on the estate for generations. Others are near the end of their careers – perhaps renting while they finish work, before moving to a place where they will live permanently during retirement. There is little local work for young people. As the estate becomes more active, Sebastian hopes that will change. 'The seasonal work that we offer at present only attracts young people who are at university. They are often children of people who used to work on the estate. When they leave, we have to rely on an older population.'

In an uncertain time for the rural economy, the object must be for Grimsthorpe to diversify away from the traditional sources of estate income – agriculture and rental property – into tourism. That will mean making more of the house. That is Emma's preserve. 'The trustees have got to the point where they are wanting to showcase what's here,' she says. Until recently, the state rooms were shown with their curtains drawn, to protect their contents. 'You couldn't genuinely see anything.' Now UV protection has been fitted to the glass, the curtains have been thrown back and the rooms transformed. 'You can look over the garden. It means more work for us: we must be constantly checking the lux levels. But it's worth it.' Next, the ropes will be coming down. 'I'd like to see people walking into one or two of the bedrooms, so they can go and feel how ghastly the horsehair mattresses used to be. We have conservators here two of three times a year; why shouldn't the public talk to them? We could put the textile conservators in the middle of the Vanbrugh Hall.'

As a charity, Grimsthorpe is not 'hungry for money,' continues Sebastian. 'It's about making a surplus so that we can then go and restore things, such as the Jupiter statue that has just been repaired, or an incredibly important sundial at Drummond which we did last year.' Recent hot summers mean that the clay on which the castle is built has dried out; cracks in the panelling are a symptom of more serious structural problems for the walls behind. 'They will be a big job to sort out.' A cushion is needed for unexpected events – such as the discovery of dry rot at Drummond which cost a million pounds to put right. 'The obvious business solution for a trust such as this is to get rid of both castles. They soak up hundreds of thousands of pounds each year. We have to fight the National Trust thing like mad. Every so often somebody says, let's give it to the National Trust and be done with it. It would be the worst solution. For me, it is so important that this house is lived in. When Lady Willoughby is here, it comes alive.'

As a child, Sebastian barely knew Grimsthorpe. His boyhood was spent at Ardverikie near Fort William and in the United States. 'Lady Willoughby had me over to stalk at Drummond every year, which was very kind of her.' He and Emma have come to Grimsthorpe with little previous knowledge but an appetite to learn. As Sebastian says, 'I know about human management because I have led soldiers. I'm not shocked or startled any more by human behaviour. I know nothing about conservation – I'm learning fast. I know nothing about farming – I'm learning fast. I know nothing about property management – I'm learning fast.'

As a result of this rapid induction, time has flown. 'I feel like we arrived yesterday. The pace has been so frenetic since we arrived, first because I like things to go quickly, and secondly, because it's such an interesting moment. Farming will change after Brexit – there's no doubt about that. Tenant law has just changed. Jane has made the generous decision to give some of her collection to the trust. This is a really important time. We have to grab it.'

Grimsthorpe looking south. In the foreground is the lake, created by
Capability Brown for the 3rd Duke of Ancaster in 1771.
Some of the woodland is hundreds of years old.

This page, Shooting is not commercially vital to
the estate but enables it to employ a gamekeeper;
wildlife does better as a result of predator control.

Opposite, Skimming pebbles on the lake. A recent
project has been to improve the water in the lake
and to clear views to and from the castle.

This page & opposite, The Chinese Drawing Room was originally a tearoom; the bow window with Gothic tracery was added in the eighteenth century. The beautiful Chinese wallpaper showing plants and animals among bamboo shoots was probably hung in 1811.

The black and gold scheme of decoration was commissioned by Eloise, Countess of Ancaster, in the 1920s.

The Tapestry Drawing Room. One of the original Tudor rooms in the castle, it was hung with Soho tapestries from Normanton Park in the 1920s by Eloise, Countess of Ancaster. The London decorating firm of Keeble Ltd created the rich chocolate colour of the walls and pilasters, heightened by gilding. Sumptuously furnished, the room is now a rare example of an intact interior scheme from between the Wars, immaculately preserved by the present Lady Willoughby d'Eresby. Lady Ancaster was the American heiress Eloise Breese.

A collection of Georgian blue john urns stands
in front of a portrait of James I from the studio
of Paul van Somer. Blue john – a corruption of
the French bleu et jaune, from its rich colours
– is a mineral only found in Derbyshire.

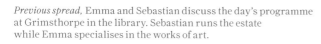

Previous spread, Emma and Sebastian discuss the day's programme at Grimsthorpe in the library. Sebastian runs the estate while Emma specialises in the works of art.

This page, The Birdcage Room (called the 'Vaulting Chamber in 1600) is decorated with *découpage* birds and trees. This and the dressing room (*opposite*) were part of the Countess of Ancaster's bedroom suite. She was the daughter of Nancy Astor.

The State Dining Room hung with early-eighteenth century
Brussels tapestries. The portrait over the chimneypiece shows
Clementina, Lady Willoughby de Eresby by Sir Thomas
Lawrence PRA. Clementina, daughter and heiress of Lord Perth,
brought Drummond Castle into the family.

This page, The ceiling was painted by Francesco Sleter
with an allegory of the Arts and Sciences, in the late 1720s,
perhaps after Vanbrugh's death in 1726 when Grimsthorpe
was being finished by Nicholas Hawksmoor. Minerva,
goddess of wisdom and the arts, greets Mercury, identified
with reason and learning (he taught Cupid to read), in the
presence of groups of related allegorical figures.

Next spread, Merlin, Emma, Sebastian and Hermione enjoy
the spatial complexity of the Vanbrugh Hall. The Italian
marble bust at Hermione's feet shows the Emperor Hadrian,

THE HISTORY OF
GRIMSTHORPE CASTLE

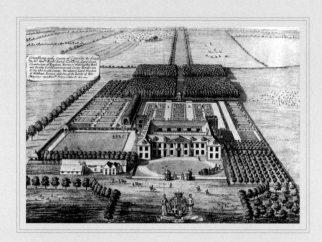

The Willoughby family has been at Grimsthorpe since the reign of Henry VIII, who granted the estate to the 11th baron Willoughby de Eresby on his marriage to one of Catherine of Aragon's ladies in waiting in 1516. Their daughter married the 1st Duke of Suffolk. Thereafter a cavalcade of noble owners came to Grimsthorpe – the Earls and later the Marquess of Lindsey, the Dukes of Ancaster and Kesteven, the Barons Gwydir and Aveland and the Earls of Ancaster. Through all these changes of ownership, the Willoughby connection was maintained, because, unusually, the barony of Willoughby de Eresby can pass through the female line. It has come into view again in the present owner, Jane Heathcote-Drummond-Willoughby, 28th Baroness Willoughby de Eresby, daughter of the 3rd Earl of Ancaster and a granddaughter of Nancy Astor, who died at Grimsthorpe in 1964.

Many of Grimsthorpe's dazzling owners enriched it, as the tide of their fortunes ebbed and flowed, and other houses in their possession came and went. But that is hardly apparent to visitors first approaching the house, seen through a splendid wrought-iron grille, surmounted by the Duke of Ancaster's coat-of-arms and the Saracen's head that is the Willoughby crest. The entrance front is all Vanbrugh, built in the early eighteenth century. Vanbrugh, however, loved castles and this is apparent in the two great towers to either side, ingeniously made to look even bigger from their position behind two smaller ones at either side of the forecourt. There is no crenellation and the towers have unmilitary Palladian windows on the first floor; but the windows of the central block have round heads, evoking an earlier period of architecture – Roman or Norman. Pairs of banded columns to either side support a massive Doric entablature.

This is an intentionally formidable building. But the skyline is playful. Instead of a central pediment is an enormous coat of arms, with statuary groups to either side. The latter show Classical ladies (Proserpina and Amphitrite) struggling in the arms of the gods (Pluto and Neptune) who are abducting them – not a fit subject for the #MeToo generation, perhaps, but suggesting a different narrative for the castle than one purely dedicated to the arts of war: the arts of love are to be celebrated behind the impenetrable privacy of its walls. Grimsthorpe had been begun by the 1st Duke of Ancaster, who died in 1723, before works were advanced; on his death, the project was immediately taken up by his son, the 2nd Duke. But Vanbrugh himself died in 1726, before his scheme for Grimsthorpe was completed. This may explain why the garden front, with its many gables and chimneystacks, remains irregular – a survival from the Tudor era. To the right is an even earlier structure: the King John's Tower, which may indeed date from the reign of King John; it was certainly built in the thirteenth century.

Tudor Grimsthorpe had been remodelled in the late seventeenth century as a Classical mansion. Surprisingly, according to a survey drawing that Vanbrugh had made before he began work, this house included a large hall, presumably created out of the Tudor great hall, though substantially enlarged. Vanbrugh converted this into the present spectacular hall, entered from a vaulted undercroft. In the hall, the architecture of round-headed arches continues that of the façade. As at Blenheim, staircases to either side rise behind arcades, to provide thrilling views of the space from different angles, although without the richness of architectural details, since there is no giant Order and the arches are the more impressive for being plain. The arches over the fireplace are filled with grisaille paintings, in imitation of statues, showing monarchs who had favoured the Willoughbys: (in order of appearance) William I, Edward III, Henry V, George I, William III, Henry VIII and Henry VII.

Relieved by little more than the ironwork of the staircase balustrade, the hall is monumental and restrained. Richness at Grimsthorpe was concentrated in the chapel.

This occupies the front part of the west wing, behind one of the Palladian windows; it is lit from three sides. A tablet in the chapel remembers Nancy Phyllis Astor, wife of the 3rd Earl of Ancaster and the mother of Lady Willoughby: 'The restoration of this chapel and much of the house was accomplished by her enthusiasm and generosity.'

The wonders of the collection at Grimsthorpe include neo-Classical furniture, family portraits, antique busts, a Flemish cabinet made of ebony and tortoiseshell and a bed upholstered with hangings made from a canopy used during the coronation of George IV in 1821. In the 1760s, the plasterer William Perritt of York worked at Grimsthorpe, probably executing the Rococo flourishes and ceiling of the Chinese Drawing Room, whose name derives from the wallpaper of birds and flowers amid bamboo shoots. The latter was probably hung in 1811. Upstairs, three Brussels tapestries from designs by Teniers can be found in the Tapestry Bedroom, where lace in the bed *à la polonaise* is supposed to have been a present from Queen Anne of Denmark when she stayed at Grimsthorpe in 1611.

If the castle is a palimpsest of many periods, whose treasures reflect the ideas and taste of the different generations who have lived at Grimsthorpe, so too is the landscape around it. Some of the woodland and individual trees are hundreds of years old. But even an exploration of the park does not exhaust Grimsthorpe's fascination, which also contains the exceptional collection of modern British art that Lady Willoughby has acquired over her lifetime. Which other country house can rival this contribution added by a twenty-first century owner to her family's long and distinguished tradition of taste and collecting?

POWDERHAM
CASTLE

Devon

Charlie, 19th Earl of Devon, and Devon's Californian countess, née Allison Joy Langer, universally known as AJ.
They are in the Belvedere Tower, a folly built by the 2nd Viscount Courtenay in the early 1770s.

The flags are out at Powderham – rainbow flags, beating in the Devon wind all along the drive to the castle. Is there a special reason for their presence? 'We often have rainbows at Powderham these days,' replies Charlie, 19th Earl of Devon. In 2008, his late father, Hugh, the 18th Earl, refused to host same sex marriages, on the grounds that it would have been against his Christian beliefs, and had the marriage licence revoked, so as not to offend against newly introduced Sexual Orientation regulations. That episode is past, forgotten. The rainbow flags are a declaration of values by Charlie and Devon's Californian countess, née Allison Joy Langer, universally known as AJ. Charlie wears a rainbow badge on his lapel. The new Powderham is inclusive.

Little about the Devons conforms to English landed stereotype. They met in a bar in Las Vegas. A recently qualified barrister, he was on tour with the London Scottish rugby club. Club loyalties meant that he was wearing a kilt. She was a golden-haired actress who had played numerous film and television roles, although Charlie knew nothing of that. She had no idea that he had been brought up in a castle, let alone was, in the words of Burke's Peerage, 'Heir Male of the historic Frankish House of Courtenay, whose pennon waved at Crecy and Agincourt and on crusade in the Holy Land' – nor would she have cared. He was 'just a beautiful man, with a sharp mind and a big heart.' They fell in love, got married and initially lived in California. It was only when Charlie's father showed signs of weakening health in 2015 that they decided to make what they thought would be an extended visit to England. Hugh's death later that year meant that they did not go back.

'For me, it's yet to feel like a home in some ways,' says AJ. This is hardly surprising. Powderham, although remodelled and softened by generations of Devons over the centuries, remains every inch a castle: an immense stone pile, with a defiantly haphazard plan. Yes, there is the charm of the rococo plasterwork, but, when the Devons moved in, Powderham did not suit family life. They had two young children, Joscelyn and Jack, but it would have been too expensive to make the house private. Says AJ, 'Much of our domestic space was open to public view. We had no barbeque in the yard, no garden furniture. We had to share our laundry with the events business. I once found my underwear in the Marble Hall.' They withdrew to the Georgian stables, only a few feet from the gatehouse but sheltered from the busy life of the estate by its own garden hedge. They expect to move back to the castle when finances and fortune allow.

There is a food festival in preparation when I arrive. It is autumn. The last time I visited, in spring, a garden festival was in full swing. These are the bookends of the Powderham season for the park; the weddings and corporate events that provide commercial income take place throughout the year. To the Devons, Powderham is, as Charlie puts it, 'simply a family business. Certainly the castle has mystique, grandeur and beauty, but it always had to be run as a business.' Handling the transition between the generations is 'what all family businesses have to do,' as well as, in due course, succession planning.

When Consuelo Vanderbilt and other American brides married into the British aristocracy at the turn of the twentieth century, they were apt to find the hierarchy of the minutely graded and omnipresent class system stultifying. In the twenty-first century, AJ barely noticed it. 'I'm an American. I'm also someone who has never been conventional. Convention is not on my radar. I'll talk to anybody the same way.' Yet if Powderham is a business, it is unlike others.

'We don't just have a five-year plan,' says AJ, 'we have a hundred-year plan.' Other businesses do not carry such a weight of expectation from, and ancient ties with, the community. Charlie isn't so sure. 'Every business has a relationship with the people it interacts with. This house is built where it's built, in the style it's built in, to communicate with the community. Originally that was people sailing up and down the river Exe – they saw this house. Now, if you want to come here and have a wedding or listen to Adam Ant, it still has that function. From the beginning, Powderham was a place to entertain, to bring people together. Sir Philip Courtenay who built this place in the fifteenth century was dependent upon having a community around him.'

To AJ, community isn't merely a buzzword but a necessity to spiritual welfare. 'Community is very important for health. 'I dealt with chronic pain growing up and found that being involved with community is one of the healthiest things you can do.' When the Devons arrived at Powderham, they asked themselves what they needed for their own health and sanity. Answer: to be connected to the community around. While Charlie went to Eton, Joscelyn and Jack attend local schools. Community will also be central to Powderham's growth, on the social enterprise model. 'Right nearby is the Eden Project,' says AJ. 'I am into Powderham being a healing space.' The Dawlish Gardens Trust, which transformed the walled garden and greenhouses while supporting people with learning difficulties and sensory problems to gain new skills, is 'very inspirational'.

The twentieth century was difficult for the estate. At the beginning of it, the family owned fifty thousand acres. This has been eroded to just three and a half thousand acres. The loss was not the result of high living but death duties and Depression. The 14th Earl of Devon died in 1927; he was succeeded by his two brothers,

both in holy orders, who died within a few months of each other in 1935. It was a sequence that, in its obituary of the 17th Earl, *The Times* likened to the film *Kind Hearts and Coronets*. The 17th Earl, Charlie's grandfather, was the son of the last brother. In 1939, he rattled society by marrying a divorcee, Venetia, who had previously been the wife of the Earl of Cottenham. With Venetia, a lady of spirit comes into the Powderham story, and as another strong and capable woman, AJ is fascinated by her. Life for Powderham's women has not always been easy, but, comments Charlie, 'they chose it.' Not so, says AJ, 'they didn't choose it. They chose a lovely man to marry and then slowly this reality dawned on them.'

Venetia's marriage took place on the eve of the Second World War and she gave birth to her fourth child, Charlie's father, on the State bed, while Exeter was being bombed. In 1943, her husband, the 17th Earl, was wounded when his helmet was hit by a bullet; he was mentioned in despatches. After the War, Venetia ran Powderham as a finishing school for girls, who were taught all aspects of housework, while, according to *The Times*, 'the Earl shot and fished'. The castle was opened to the public in 1959. Visitors came in their thousands; but the income could hardly compensate for the toll taken by the triple death duties at rates of forty and fifty per cent. When Charlie inherited, Powderham was in a 'much better state than it had been'. But the roof has still to be fixed.

Hence the Devons' business-oriented approach. 'We have been selling capital for three generations,' says Charlie. 'We want to turn that around. We are going from begrudgingly sharing the house to very enthusiastically sharing it; that's a big shift.' They want to create a business that grows. 'I've got a silly fantasy of buying back some of the Courtenay castles that have left the family,' says Charlie – although he admits that they are in some cases happily occupied by other owners. He continues to work for half the week as a barrister; AJ remains an actor, whatever the demands of children and Powderham for the time being.

And another job has come into Charlie's portfolio: recently he was elected as one of the crossbench hereditary peers in the House of Lords. 'It's not an opportunity available to many people', admits Charlie. As a lawyer and historian, he was fascinated. 'I try to sit two days a week. There's a lot to learn.'

You do not have to be specially sensitive to body language to realise that AJ isn't delighted. 'It's great for him – he gets to run off to London and fulfil his dream of entering the House of Lords. We stay here, my kids are still young.' These are not unfamiliar issues, though given an edge by AJ's experience. 'I was very independent when I met Charlie. He came to my house in California. I was working, he could study. We were ensconced in a very diverse community. He was my hippy, feminist husband. On the day of his father's memorial service, it was like *The Godfather*: there was a line going through the castle and around the courtyard of people wanting to come and pay their respects and shake his hand. All of a sudden, he takes on the patriarchy. He's speaking to me in ways I've never experienced.' She is acutely conscious of the mental health implications of the responsibility of Charlie's position. 'Because of this image of what an earl is, it can be a monster. It can take good men and convince them they aren't enough as they are.'

Primogeniture is another 'fun subject,' according to Charlie. For him, as for others in his position, the consequences can be oppressive. 'You become your father. You get his name, and his cufflinks,

and you shave in his sink.' Unlike many of the other country houses, Powderham is not held by a trust. There are obvious advantages to the freedom that outright ownership gives – but with it comes also a burden. 'Being sole owner you feel you have to be a specialist in every department.' Trustees give expertise and impartial support.

Estates like Powderham have only survived because they have not been split among siblings on inheritance. The answer, for the Devons, is to create a big enough operation for both children. 'Philip, who built Powderham, was the sixth son of the 2nd Earl,' notes Charlie. 'It was a business that was growing. He was planted as the head of a cadet branch in a new location.'

Succession is, in one sense, the only exit strategy for a business like Powderham, which it would be unthinkable to sell. But 'it was never our intention to live here full-time,' says AJ. 'The ambition is to establish a business we can run from anywhere.' The children love Powderham but California also has a place in their lives. 'No one before my father and grandfather expected to be here all the time,' explains Charlie. 'It was a major feature of their lives but not their sole purpose. Richard Courtenay, Bishop of Norwich, was with Henry V at the siege of Harfleur.'

If Powderham does not quite feel like home to its new chatelaine, AJ has found that 'you do fall in love with it.' Though the size of the place, the history and the number of estate buildings in need of attention, make it also 'a very large enigma.'

Ceiling of Powderham's exuberant staircase hall, made in the mid-1750s by a team of otherwise unknown craftsmen, led by John Jenkins.

This page & opposite, Powderham Castle from the north-east. The low ground in front of the castle was once covered by the estuary of the River Exe; there was a courtyard and gatehouse on this side. Deer still graze the ancient deer park, first shown on a map in 1723.

Next spread, The family in the arches of the American Garden Pavillion: AJ, Jack, Joscelyn and Charlie. The children go to local schools: community, says AJ, is essential for well-being.

Coats of arms on the fireplace of the State Dining Room, created by the architect Charles Fowler in the 1840s for the 10th Earl of Devon. The Earl had inherited from a second cousin. It was during his period that the railway arrived and the castle was turned to face inland.

In 1861 the medieval Grange was converted into a family chapel.

Previous spread, The Marble Hall, with portraits of Charlie, his parents and sisters around the enormous Powderham clock by William Stumbels of Totnes circa 1752.

This page, Music is important in this family. AJ plays the guitar to Joscelyn in the White Drawing Room.

Opposite, Jack on sax.

In the mid-1750s John Jenkins, assisted by William Brown and Stephen Coney, were employed to turn the staircase hall into what Mark Girouard described in *Country Life* (July 11, 1963) as one of the most vibrant examples of Rococo plasterwork in England.

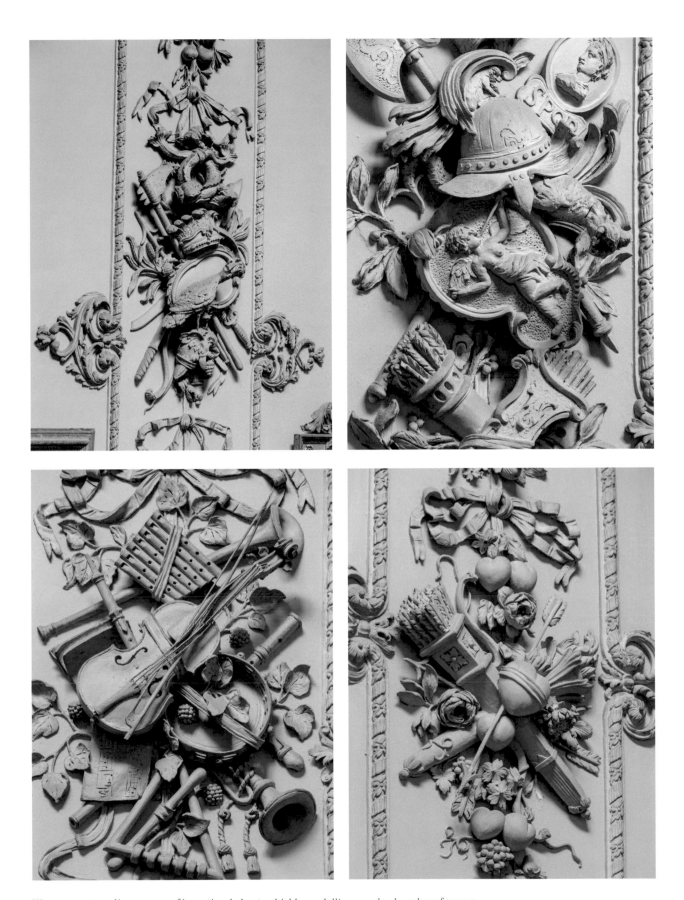

We see an extraordinary range of invention: helmets, shields, medallions, apples, bunches of grapes, violins, Pan pines, oboes, arrows in quivers and much else, all suspended from bows of waving ribbon. The craftsmanship is of the highest order.

Opposite, A walk in the autumn woods.
The spiritual value of Nature is important.

This Page, Joscelyn helps Charlie raise
the family flag.

THE HISTORY OF POWDERHAM CASTLE

Until the mid-eighteenth century, Powderham Castle cast its eyes proudly on the river Exe, facing it with a gatehouse and walled courtyard that were demolished for the Georgian landscaping of the park. When the castle – strictly a fortified manor house – was built around 1400, by a younger branch of the powerful Courtenay Family, Earls of Devon, it was easier to travel by sea and river than by road, and the Exe, leading from Exmouth and Exeter, was an important trading route. In 1455, as Devon magnates jockeyed for position at the beginning of the Wars of the Roses, Powderham was besieged by the Earl of Devon, since its lord, Sir Philip Courtenay, had allied himself with the rival Bonville family; the lifting of the siege by the Bonvilles caused the Battle of Clyst Heath outside Exeter, one of the last private battles on English soil. (All the male representatives of the senior Devon line were subsequently beheaded or killed later in the Wars of the Roses.) During the English Civil War, Powderham stood out for the King; it was captured for Parliament in 1646 and its then owner, Sir William Courtenay, who had been wounded fighting for the Royalists in

Somerset, abandoned it, in favour of his wife's more up-to-date Forde House at Newton Abbott.

When a later Sir William Courtenay and his wife, Lady Anne Bertie, returned to Powderham around 1710, they remodelled it, starting a tradition of adding rooms in and around the medieval core that continued for a century and a half. The original building had been long and thin, with various projections; this was extended to the north and east, attaching drawing rooms and libraries that could be reached from a Marble Hall and staircase created within the medieval great hall. The man responsible appears to have been John Moyle of Exeter, a master builder and bricklayer.

Sir William's son, also Sir William, inherited in 1735 and became 1st Viscount Powderham in 1762. A memory of the Baroque splendour with which he enriched Powderham in the 1730s remains in a pair of sumptuous rosewood bookcases, decorated with gilded capitals and garlands. But taste moved on, and in the mid-1750s John Jenkins, assisted by

William Brown and Stephen Coney, were employed to turn the staircase hall into what Mark Girouard described in *Country Life* (July 11, 1963) as one of 'the half-dozen or so most sumptuous surviving examples of Rococo plasterwork in England. It is as though the Palladian barriers had suddenly broken down and a tremendous Rococo floor came sweeping into the castle, leaving, when it had subsided, an extraordinary and wonderful miscellany of objects thickly encrusted on walls and ceilings.' Although Jenkins was a craftsman of the highest order, nothing else is known of him. We can only say that his assistants came from London, since their travel expenses are entered in the accounts.

The 3rd Viscount came of age in 1789, the year after his father the 2nd Viscount's death. Christened William but known by some as Kitty Courtenay, he had been a famously beautiful boy and, at twenty-one, he was a handsome young man, painted by Richard Cosway in masquerade dress (a gold cloak and enrichments over a van Dyke suit of black velvet) for his coming of age ball. For the first time in the family's history, he went to a nationally famous architect, James Wyatt, to build a large music room at the north-east corner of the castle. The style is simpler and more monumental than that in which Wyatt had begun his career twenty years earlier, under the influence of Robert Adam. The fireplace by Richard Westmacott is flanked by full-length Greek shepherd and dancing girl playing respectively a flute and tambourine. Furniture supplied by Marsh and Tatham at the end of the 1790s has arms supported by dolphins, the Courtenay crest.

The 3rd Viscount was a homosexual who loved beauty. In 1784, when he was sixteen, his relationship with the writer and art collector William Beckford, eight years his senior, had forced the latter to leave England for an extended period.

This did not stop the 3rd Viscount's homosexual behaviour and in 1810 he was also hounded out of the country for gross indecency. Nevertheless, by the time of his death in Paris in 1835, the 3rd Viscount had succeeded in reviving the earldom of Devon, making him the 9th Earl. His body was buried at Powderham.

The big bay of the music room looked out over a landscape that had changed completely from the watery scene of the Middle Ages. During the eighteenth century, the marshes had been drained and planted with fine timber. Whereas before the estuary had come right up to the castle, an expanse of park now ran for several hundred yards down to the water, the distant view of which added to the beauties of the situation.

In the 1840s, the 3rd Viscount's cousin and heir, the 10th Earl, employed the Devon-born architect Charles Fowler to reinvent Powderham: with railway having replaced river as the most convenient mode of transport, the Castle was turned to face inland. A battlemented gatehouse opens into a new courtyard; a Tudor-style banqueting hall was created on the west front. If Powderham had not quite been a castle in the medieval period, it undoubtedly was now. And if that closed the chapter on the architecture of the house, it opened another on the challenge of maintaining it, a theme of castle life since the Second World War. Charlie and AJ are now the twenty-eighth generation to be living in what they describe as 'this remarkable family home.'

INVERARAY CASTLE

Argyll

The Duke and Duchess of Argyll (Eleanor and Torquhil), in the Campbell tartan.
They stand in front of one of the trophies of arms in the Armoury Hall of Inveraray Castle, Argyll.

The Segways are kept by the door. Charlotte, aged eleven, says that she's not allowed to use them on the ground floor in case she bumps into anything precious but it's fair game in the basement, with its stone corridors. She walks off across the hall on stilts. There are advantages to growing up in Inveraray Castle, home to the Duke and Duchess of Argyll.

Inveraray is one of the great showpieces of Britain. Towered and turreted, the castle rises against a background of forest and mountain; in front of it is Loch Fyne, fringed by one of the military roads built after the 1745 Jacobite Rebellion (as Protestants, the Dukes of Argyll were on the side of the Hanoverian Kings – hence the fortune that allowed them to build on this princely scale.)

The Campbells are known to have been in Argyll since the twelfth century. They built a castle but by the time Archibald, 3rd Duke of Argyll inherited the estate in 1743, deep 'rents' had appeared in the wall and it was too expensive to restore. Consequently, a new castle was built by the London architect Roger Morris, to a symmetrical scheme that may not have been authentically Gothic but was an early example of Georgian castle design. The bluish green stone with which it was faced – chloritic schist, to geologists – came from further down the loch, while the inside of the walls is made of local granite. Work lasted sixty years.

Inveraray has been a magnet for visitors since it was built. Dr Johnson came, finding it 'a stately place.' Keats came, appalled by the 'horrors of a solo on the Bag-pipe'. Dorothy Wordsworth came ... as did many others. Today, Inveraray is one of the biggest private tourist attractions in Scotland, open seven days a week during the six-month season. Visitors numbers have doubled to a hundred and twenty thousand since Torquhil,

the present Duke of Argyll, inherited in 2001. (The filming of the *Downton Abbey* two-hour 2012 Christmas special at Inveraray helped.) Cruise ships that dock at Oban or in the Clyde may send fourteen coaches at a time. 'Glasgow now has flights from Iceland, the Middle East and Beijing. The rooms have information sheets in Mandarin.'

As a result, the family must co-exist with holidaymaking crowds. In an age when privacy is, for most homeowners, a domestic ideal – indeed a necessity – the Argylls are, despite being able to slip in and out through a special family door at the side of the house, often on show. Torquhil actively enjoys meeting the public; 'it's a privilege,' he says. 'They're usually so thrilled to meet me, particularly the Americans.' Admittedly, they do not always know that they have met him. Dressed in a rugby shirt or all-enveloping rainwear, he is sometimes mistaken for one of the castle staff. His wife Eleanor, née Cadbury, finds that it can be 'a bit intrusive' on occasion. 'You have to learn to keep quiet at times. Once or twice I've started to shout at the children and then stopped. But look at it from the visitors' perspective: it makes their day. There are times when I'm really busy but I'll always go out and have a selfie taken.'

Charlotte and her two brothers, Archie and Rory – or Lady Charlotte Campbell, the Marquess of Lorne and Lord Rory Campbell, to give them their proper titles – are not always in the mood to be stopped, as they often are in the summer months, by visitors who have seen their photographs on a tour of the house. Their mother tells them 'you just have to share with people. There are lots of bonuses. We can fit a billiard table and a ping pong table into the playroom. Not many people get to have a playroom that large.' For Torquhil's fiftieth birthday, forty-three people sat down to dinner;

all of them could stay in the house except for a handful put up by his mother. When Eleanor invites ninety local children to tea at Christmas, she can feed them all in her tearoom. Of course, castle life has its inconveniences, but they are not always quite what you would suppose. There is the dinner party issue. 'In seventeen years of marriage, we've only been out to about two dinner parties.' Inveraray is too remote. 'On the other hand, we just invite people here. There are five of us, so we're not that welcome in so many other houses, because of the space we take up.' Torquhil and Eleanor are hands-on parents, unlike previous generations of the aristocracy. Supermarkets do now deliver to Inveraray– if the order is placed three weeks in advance. So the Argylls must be organised. Packages from Amazon Prime do not arrive the next day, as they would in a city: it might take them a week. 'My cheese for a corporate dinner came from Glasgow the other day. They put it on a lorry on Monday; I got a message saying it would arrive on Friday at 6pm. I told them not to bother.' Not much food is grown at the castle, since the walled garden with its Victorian greenhouse is in ruins.

Although, by anyone's standards, the castle is large, it is not ideally planned to accommodate family life in the busy summer months. In the very centre is the towering Armoury Hall; so it is difficult to cross from one side of the building to the other without being seen. Previous generations overcame the problem by simply closing the castle – for example, in the middle of the day, when Torquhil's father progressed from his study to the dining room to eat luncheon. Every Friday Inveraray would be closed for cleaning. On Sundays it did not open until 2pm to allow people to go to church. Modern business thinking dictates a different regime.

But another change is that Inveraray is now the family's home throughout the year.

When I visit over the autumn half term, the children are industriously carving pumpkin lanterns. It used to be that the castle was only occupied in the summer months. So an innovation of cardinal importance has been the new heating system. During the winter, Inveraray used to be seriously cold. No longer: a hundred and twenty-four radiators have been fitted to keep the family rooms at a good temperature (although there can still be a perceptible chill in the State rooms). Numerous diamond-tipped saw blades were worn out in the effort to cut through the hard granite walls to fit pipework. But the result has justified the work, according to Eleanor: 'I grew up in London, Gloucestershire and Cape Town; I've got very thin blood.' Although her Quaker heritage does not allow her to dwell on the sybaritic aspect for long. Central heating allows the castle to 'work harder now. We can put people up, have more events.'

And yet even the most public space in the castle – the great Armoury Hall – has an intimate dimension for those who live here. Four years ago it was redecorated. 'This was a massive project,' remembers Torquhil. 'It required fifty tons of scaffolding and eight hundred litres of paint. Every single piece of armour had to be taken down and cleaned.' The last time the arms and armour had been cleaned was in 1975, when they were lacquered in line with the preservation thinking of the time. The lacquer had gone yellow over time. 'We had a gun cleaning station. If anyone had a spare half an hour, in they went. It was a fascinating project: we learnt so much about the amazing things that we have. Before it had seemed just a whole lot of stuff on the wall.' One discovery was the sword that Big Duncan Mackenzie of Ballachulish had wielded at the Battle of Prestonpans, slicing through the helmet and head of a Hanoverian soldier. It was identified by the dent it had in it. Every activity on the estate must 'sweat'.

This is true not just of the castle but of each department on the seventy-five-thousand-acre estate – caravan parks, agriculture, forestry, residential property, sporting activities, and the different forms of green energy: wind, hydro and biomass. 'If it doesn't sweat, it won't survive,' says Torquhil. Like other owners, he views the castle as one among other stand-alone businesses – although one with a special dynamic. 'It's the bit that I spend a huge amount of time on – a disproportionate time. It's our public face.' It means that the Argylls live not so much above the shop as in the shop. Torquhil studied at Cirencester – now the Royal Agricultural University. When he inherited and the old trust ran out, it was decided not to reappoint trustees. Before that, he travelled widely abroad as an ambassador for the drinks company Pernod Ricard, a role that he has retained for fifty days a year. Moving to Argyll and Bute required a change of perspective. It was not, though, towards farming; 'even though I trained in agriculture, we have scaled back our own operation. This is very marginal land. Getting tenant farmers to come in to replace ones who are retiring or going out is getting more and more difficult.'

Torquhil married Eleanor in 2002. She has embraced Inveraray life, running events, the tearoom and shop. 'During the summer,' she says, 'it's all hands on deck – though we're fortunate that the estate is big enough to own part of Tiree. We can jump ship every now and then and go off for a fortnight – it's not very far.' What she calls 'flash holidays' are out. There are no smart sports cars at the castle, except when other people bring them for rallies. Her usual shopping destination for clothes is the Gretna Gateway Outlet Village.

The team at Inveraray is 'lean', but nevertheless amounts to twenty-eight permanent and thirty-eight temporary staff. This makes the castle a major local employer. One of the economic constraints in Argyll and Bute is the shortage of places to live, so the estate is seeking to add three hundred houses to Inveraray. Room guides at the castle often come from the ranks of the retirees who have come to Argyll and Bute after professional careers; 'they are often good at history, good at languages and can work the tills.'

In theory, the Argylls should be just the sort of people that a certain kind of politician should hate. English accents raise hackles. But even those who are, in other circumstances, ideologically opposed to lairds generally come to a grudging acceptance of the contribution that Inveraray and its family make to this remote part of the British Isles, suffering from depopulation and lack of jobs. Tourism is the principle source of employment, and 'people would have little reason to come if it weren't for the castle,' says Torquhil.

Planning can be an issue, and not every project proposed by the estate obtains the necessary consents. Torquhil, though, is relaxed. 'My family has been here for centuries.' This is celebrated in the Argyll Papers, one of the most important private archives in the country, which has just been housed in a specially equipped centre in the castle's former stable yard. 'We are in it for the long term. If for some reason I can't do something, my son will do it. Does it matter if I do it today, or if I do it in thirty years' time? Not really.'

Archie Campbell, the Marquess of Lorne, by a rushing
Highland burn. In younger days, he served as a
Page of Honour to H.M. the Queen.

Previous spread,
Inveraray Castle, on
the bank of Loch Fyne.
It was begun by the
3rd Duke of Argyll in
1744. After the Jacobite
rebellion the next year,
General Wade built the
military road beside the
loch; the bridge is by the
architect and engineer
Robert Mylne, who also
worked at the castle.

Today, the seventy-five-
thousand-acre estate
includes agriculture,
forestry, residential
property, sporting
activities, caravan parks
and the different forms
of green energy: wind,
hydro and biomass.

Eating, then and now. *Opposite*, The 5th Duke commissioned Robert Mylne to decorate the State Dining Room, as part of an association with Mylne that lasted – despite Mylne's prickly temperament – for thirty years. The French artists Girard and Guinand completed the painting scheme in 1784. Made in Paris by Dupasquier, the chairs still have their original Beauvais tapestry upholstery.

This page, Charlotte sits at the family dining room, near the kitchen.

This page, The Tapestry Drawing Room, with the Beauvais tapestries made for it in the 1780s. Above the chimneypiece is John Hoppner's portrait of Lady Charlotte Campbell as Aurora, dancing on the clouds and strewing flowers in the air. She was the younger daughter of the 5th Duke and his beautiful wife, Elizabeth Gunning, who had been previously married to the Duke of Hamilton.

Opposite, Robert Mylne had the ceilings for Inveraray made in London out of papier mâché.

Charlotte practises the
piano in the Saloon.

In the centre of the castle, the Armoury Hall is seventy feet high. When it was painted a few years ago, the project required fifty tons of scaffolding and eight hundred litres of paint. Among the discoveries when the arms were cleaned – every piece by hand – was the sword that Big Duncan Mackenzie of Ballachulish had wielded at the Battle of Prestonpans, slicing through the helmet and head of a Hanoverian soldier; it was identified by the dent it had in it.

Opposite, The covered entrance to the castle, erected to mark the marriage in 1871 of the future 9th Duke of Argyll to Princess Louise, daughter of Queen Victoria. Today, a signpost is needed to direct visitors.

This page, Argyll monogram and Campbell emblem of a boar's head on the new gates.

This page, Charlotte, Rory and Torquhil in the woods. Bonfires are a popular family activity.

Opposite, Crossing the stepping stones in the river.

On the battlements of the castle, Torquhil contemplates the future. 'If for some reason I can't do something, my son will do it. Does it matter if I do it today, or if I do it in thirty years' time? Not really.'

THE HISTORY OF
INVERARAY CASTLE

Three white posts in the ground mark the site of the old Inveraray Castle. It had been the ancient stronghold of the Campbell chiefs, who had been living – and dominating – Argyll since at least the days of Great Colin Campbell in the thirteenth century. But by the 1740s, this venerable pile had become uninhabitable; it was certainly unworthy of a family who were now Dukes, the 10th Earl of Argyll having been raised to the Dukedom by William III in 1701. In 1743, the impetuous 2nd Duke of Argyll, a soldier who rarely visited his Highland estates, died, leaving five daughters but no son. His brother Archibald, 3rd Duke, inherited Inveraray, along with large tracts of western and central Scotland and several islands. Duke Archibald was sixty-one and, as a lawyer and politician, a decidedly different figure from his brother. Although a widower for twenty years and without legitimate children, he immediately applied himself to the improvement of his estates, including Inveraray Castle, which he had not seen since defending it against the Jacobite Rebellion of 1715.

Previously Duke Archibald had lived mainly in London. Before even visiting Inveraray, he hatched schemes to improve the castle, the town at its gates and life on his estates. Even travelling to Inveraray was a challenge, involving either a hazardous sea voyage or a trek across the mountains. Plans for a visit were made but long delayed, although Duke Archibald – 'slovenly and bookish', according to Horace Walpole – loved architecture and the planning of gardens. He became increasingly anxious to see Inveraray in person: 'curiosity alone if it were not my Love of laying out Grounds & Gardening would draw me thither, especially considering, that I have now done with Political Ambition.' A survey was made of the castle but there were, the mason reported, 'Large Rents in both Side walls' and 'In most Places it is Greatly Shattered.' When the Duke succeeded in reaching Inveraray from Edinburgh in 1744, the London architect Roger Morris was in his retinue. The next year, at the outbreak of the 1745 Rebellion, the Duke had to hurry back to London so fast that friction caused the axle of his coach to catch fire.

But works had been set in train at Inveraray that would last for sixty years.

Morris designed a new castle from an initial drawing by Vanbrugh, one hundred feet, with towers at each corner and a central tower. It is surrounded by a fosse, crossed by two bridges. Instead of being a courtyard, the central space is a hall that rises seventy feet from the floor; it is lit by pointed windows in the central tower. With its turrets and crenellations, Inveraray is certainly a castle, although really like a medieval one. Near the castle – but not so near that the Dukes could see it – the town of Inveraray was rebuilt on model lines. In 1758, the minister of the church, Alexander Carlyle, stayed at the inn there, but took his meals with Duke Archibald. Carlyle has left an attractive description of the elderly Duke, who 'waived ceremony very much, and took no trouble at table, and would not let himself be waited for, and came in when he pleased, and sat down on the chair that was left, which was neither at the head nor foot of the table.' There were fifteen or sixteen people at the dinner table. 'After the ladies were withdrawn and he had drunk his bottle of claret, he retired to an easy-chair set hard by the fireplace: drawing a black silk nightcap over his eyes, he slept, or seemed to sleep, for an hour and a half.'

William Adam acted as the supervising architect at Inveraray. But when the Duke died seventeen years after beginning the Castle, he had still not been able to sleep in it. Many of the principal rooms had no floors and the hall had only received its first coat of plaster. It was left to John, the 5th Duke, who inherited in 1770, to complete the Castle. He employed Robert Mylne as his architect. Mylne, having travelled widely in France and Italy, had his first great success as the architect of Blackfriars Bridge in London.

Thereafter he was as much in demand as an engineer as an architect, and he built several bridges at Inveraray during an association with Duke John that lasted thirty years (remarkably, perhaps, in view of Mylne's prickly temperament). He also fitted out the castle in an elegant and magnificent style. Mylne's pointed arches were internally disguised with rounded-headed sash windows. Ceiling decorations were designed and supplied from London, apparently in a kind of papier mâché. The Saloon was hung with Beauvais tapestries that the Duke and his Duchess had commissioned in Paris.

In 1877, fire struck the castle and Anthony Salvin came to restore it, taking the opportunity to add an extra story and witches' hat turrets; this created a more romantic profile, of the kind seen at Balmoral. Fire broke out again in 1975; fortunately the speed and dedication of the 12th Duke to begin an immediate restoration saved even the delicate painted decoration in the main rooms.

Two years earlier, in 1973, the 11th Duke had died just as the splendid *Inverary and the Dukes of Argyll* by Ian Lindsay and Mary Cosh was being finished. In his foreword, the Duke explained how the 'crushing burden of Death Duties on my succession made it a question whether or not the restoration of the Castle and Town could be undertaken.' But even the 1975 fire did not overwhelm the family, and Inveraray exemplifies the spirit of resurgence which is the theme of this book.

MADRESFIELD COURT

www.MadresfieldEstate.co.uk

LOSELEY PARK

www.LoseleyPark.co.uk

HELMINGHAM HALL

www.Helmingham.com

BURTON AGNES HALL

www.BurtonAgnes.com

HUTTON-IN-THE-FOREST

www.Hutton-in-the-Forest.co.uk

DODDINGTON HALL

www.DoddingtonHall.com

BROUGHTON CASTLE

www.BroughtonCastle.com

HOPETOUN HOUSE

www.Hopetoun.co.uk

FIRLE PLACE

www.Firle.com

GRIMSTHORPE CASTLE

www.Grimsthorpe.co.uk

POWDERHAM CASTLE

www.Powderham.co.uk

INVERARAY CASTLE

www.Inveraray-Castle.com

BEHIND THE LENS

By Dylan Thomas

Home has taken on a new meaning since photographing this book. Production is being finished at a time of lockdown during the Coronavirus crisis of 2020, when Britain is spending rather more time at home than it would like. This makes me remember the carefree days (as they now seem) spent travelling from one country house to another for *Old Homes, New Life* with particular pleasure – every one of these magical places was a delight. The Englishman's home is figuratively his castle (although some of the houses in this book really are castles); now it has become a fortress against disease, with callers kept at an obligatory two metres distance. So I appreciate all the more the generosity with which I was received and the freedom I was given to roam through this selection of a dozen country houses, full of artworks and personal memorabilia, more or less at will. So a huge thank you to the owners and their families, all of whom were hospitable to a fault. What happy pre-Coronavirus days!

The project began under the dome of Tate Britain, eating a quiche with Clive Aslet. 'You know, Dylan, you ought to think of doing a book,' he said. I replied: 'Yes, let's' – and we were off. First it was an early start for the drive up the A1 to Doddington Hall. This is the home of James and Claire Birch, and James is the President of the Historic Houses Association: the champion of a progressive attitude to a deeply traditional Old World. We discussed our proposed list with him, he added other names, we honed it down from several dozen to twelve and made our preparatory visits. Within a month I had started to photograph.

If anyone had reservations about having this intruder in their midst, they were too polite to show it, and I was given unrestricted access from State Room to boot room.

On average, I spent three days at each property. I wanted to do this project alone, without an assistant. This came from the many years I spent working with Lord Snowdon who would always say that you can make someone feel relaxed when you photograph them - or very uncomfortable; so best keep the team to the bare minimum. I took that to heart. Maybe, going solo, I went a little too far. Homeowners had to help me bounce light from my reflectors around rooms. As far as possible I used natural light, although when the weather was very British, they also lent a hand setting up flash lighting to brighten the darkest corners. I showed them how to straighten bedside lamps using a small stack of coins (most of which I then forgot to remove: perhaps they will still be there to puzzle future house archaeologists). I can only apologise for all the times I called a child by the wrong name. On one occasion it was the dog's name. The twins at Loseley, Rocco and Aubrey, kept swapping their clothes, just to confuse me further.

I daresay I had a critical audience. Cressida Inglewood herself worked as a photographer in London before becoming the chatelaine of Hutton-in-the-Forest: I was being watched by a pro. In the splendid hall of Madresfield Court, there were so many photographs in frames that I realised each family would need to be formally recorded. My problem at Madresfield was the library; with so many books I had to sit down and ponder the world. A dust free library – how do they do it? I daresay Colin Lee, who has worked there since before Clive's first visit in 1981, would know.

One of the joys of the project has been to discover the great plans each family has for the future. These lovely people are not intimidated by their situation as custodians of big and important country houses, which are hardly cheap or easy to run and finance. Sophia and Alexander have entered into their time at Loseley with gusto. I enjoyed the theatricality of this shoot, which involved many changes of clothes for the participants – although a parcel of Alexander's freshly laundered shirts did not arrive until I was leaving the house. Helmingham also has a new generation installed. My challenge was to photograph a giant game of pick up sticks, played between two competitive boys. By the end of the shoot, the jar of Maltesers was nearly empty. Ralph was hoping for a record-breaking catch when I photographed him fishing in the moat. Ed said he had done the same thing as a child. On Sunday evening, dinner is smoked salmon and scrambled eggs – what a heavenly way to start the week. (And Sophie, thank you again for that roast chicken with crispy bacon. Fabulous.)

There was an attic to renovate at Hopetoun while I was there; Skye was meeting with architects and plumbers. At Inveraray, Torquhil and I went further with – for someone with no great head for heights – a never-to-be-forgotten climb up fire escapes onto the roof. The country-house attic, even the country-house roof should be subjects in themselves. So is the country house on the cinema screen. Firle was being transformed into a film set for *Emma* when we first visited. 'Should we redecorate and put the colour back to the original,' they were wondering, 'or keep it as they've done it?' Questions of that kind don't come up in my world very often. Horses are big at Firle but the riding school smells not of hay but baking: it is set up with display kitchens for *Bake Off: The Professionals*. The cakes sold in the tea room are also spectacular.

'Can I get you a coffee? Help yourself to anything,' said Martin, when I was staying at Broughton Castle. It would have felt like a complete home from home, had it not been for the size of the bedroom. Martin makes Broughton come alive. While professing not to know about roses, he seems to have the name of every single one (and there are a lot) in his memory. His Kiftsgate rose is the biggest I've ever seen. There was a shoot on when I was photographing the boys in their punt: a wounded duck flew overhead and expired on the water a couple of feet from the boat. That's the country, for you.

So many of these country houses – Burton Agnes, for example – are a sight to behold from a drone. But always it is the warmth of the hospitality on the ground that I shall remember. Thank you to everyone for making me welcome, and the smiles and laughter along the way.

This page and opposite,
The snapper snapped.
Dylan with his able
assistant Charlotte
photographs Archie,
who photographs
him back.

This page, Lucy Chenevix-Trench talks to Clive in the kitchen at Madresfield Court.

Opposite, Dylan and Clive taking life seriously at a country house in Devon. The Adam and Eve sculpture is by Emily Young.

ACKNOWLEDGEMENTS

This book has been one of the most enjoyable of our professional lives and we have many people to thank, above all the inhabitants of these extraordinary houses who made us so welcome. Families have not only flung open their doors for us but open-handedly given of their time and hospitality; and that is even kinder when one considers how much work it is to run a country house and the businesses that support it. Without their generosity, this book would have been nothing.

Old Homes, New Life has been completed during the strange and unprecedented conditions of the Coronavirus lockdown of 2020. We now think back to those visits around Britain – along motorways and country roads, by train and taxi, following map and SatNav – with a mix of nostalgia and disbelief. Was it possible to travel freely to so many beautiful places without restriction or to roam at will around extensive gardens and landscape parks? We have the evidence in the photographs Dylan took. We find them inspiring as well as pleasurable. What crises, national and domestic, have rocked the world during the lifetime of these country houses. They have lived through plague, world wars, family tragedy and scandal: very bad times indeed. And yet they got through them. This makes them symbols of both endurance and hope. 'Resurgence' is a big word and not to be used lightly but it's what we see in these houses – and we are uplifted.

We have other thanks to express. To Kate Turner, the production manager of Triglyph Books; to Jeff Knowles and Nick Hard, for their ineffable design skills; and to our families for tolerance of our absences around the country. They may not have believed us when we said it was really hard work.

We won't be able to list all the happy memories we have taken away but can't leave the subject without signaling special gratitude to:

Lucy and Jonathan at Madresfield for finding a black iPhone lost on the ebony of a grand piano;

Alexander and Sophia at Loseley for the sound of children in the kitchen (country houses shouldn't be too quiet);

Edward and Sophie at Helmingham for sharing their Sunday evening smoked salmon and scrambled eggs;

Simon and Olivia at Burton Agnes for the exuberance of a house full of music;

Richard and Cressida at Hutton-in-the-Forest for the idea for the book, evolved over a Potfest weekend;

James and Claire at Doddington for so many introductions to country houses and families, all of whom were sure-fire suggestions;

Martin and Pauline at Broughton for pheasant and game stew served beneath a fourteenth-century vault;

Andrew and Skye at Hopetoun for the dragonflies in the walled garden;

Gages of all ages at Firle for horses amid the fairytale beauty of their Sussex estate;

Sebastian and Emma at Grimsthorpe for an unquenchably can-do attitude;

Charlie and AJ at Powderham for the four-wheel drive that got Dylan over the temporary moat around the castle, when the river Kenn burst its banks;

Torquhil and Eleanor at Inveraray for scaling fire ladders up to the roof.

Dylan Thomas and Clive Aslet
April 2020

THE PUBLISHER

Triglyph Books is a collaboration between the photographer Dylan Thomas and the writer Clive Aslet. Dylan has extensive experience of photographing portraits and architecture, having worked for several years with Lord Snowdon. One of Clive's specialist subjects is the country house; he was architectural editor of *Country Life*, then, for thirteen years, editor of that magazine, and he has also published many books on the subject. It seemed natural that Dylan and Clive should create a book together. *Old Homes, New Life* is the result.

The idea has been to look at country houses as they are, in all their splendour, today. Country houses are an extraordinary feature of the British scene and excite much public interest. But they can be misunderstood. Visitors are apt to see them as mouldering piles, or bastions of privilege, as repositories of fabulous collections, with great cultural resonance, or as symbols of various kinds of repression. They may be all those things. But they are also family homes. It has been our joy and privilege to meet the people who live in the dozen houses we have featured and lift the ropes that separate public from private. We found that each one of them was different; each faced the future in different ways.

There was another thing. We had a lot of fun doing it. So much so that we did not want to entrust the result to a commercial publisher; we decided to form our own publishing house, Triglyph Books. (A triglyph, incidentally, is an element in Classical architecture. We cannot quite agree how it should be pronounced.) This, we felt, was all very well as a means of putting our own projects before the public, but good secrets need to be shared. We have therefore offered our services to the public. So far, we have several projects on hand from architects such as Oliver Cope Architect in New York and ADAM Architecture in Winchester. Others are in development. We would like to thank our friends for their support of our fledgling brand. We hope their books give them as much pleasure and excitement as they are giving us.

We think there is a space for Triglyph to occupy in bespoke publishing. We specialise in the small and beautifully formed. We have between us a deep knowledge of luxury markets. We are obsessive about quality of presentation. We work with London's best designers; we understand every nuance of photography and illustrations. We dot i's, we cross t's. Publishing is an exhilaration more than a job. In this age of rapidly changing technology, it pays to be nimble. As a small, indeed micro-sized company, Triglyph can produce books quicker than old-fashioned firms with rigid production schedules and big overheads. We enjoy the interface with our clients. We offer a personal service.

This book celebrates the future of the country house. It also marks the birth of Triglyph Books. We hope the prospects are fair for both. We shall report back in a hundred years' time.